Modern
American
Painting

**TIME LIFE BOOKS ®**

*Other Publications:*

WORLD WAR II

THE GREAT CITIES

HOME REPAIR AND IMPROVEMENT

THE WORLD'S WILD PLACES

THE TIME-LIFE LIBRARY OF BOATING

HUMAN BEHAVIOR

THE ART OF SEWING

THE OLD WEST

THE EMERGENCE OF MAN

THE AMERICAN WILDERNESS

THE TIME-LIFE ENCYCLOPEDIA OF GARDENING

LIFE LIBRARY OF PHOTOGRAPHY

THIS FABULOUS CENTURY

FOODS OF THE WORLD

TIME-LIFE LIBRARY OF AMERICA

GREAT AGES OF MAN

LIFE SCIENCE LIBRARY

THE LIFE HISTORY OF THE UNITED STATES

TIME READING PROGRAM

LIFE NATURE LIBRARY

LIFE WORLD LIBRARY

FAMILY LIBRARY:

    HOW THINGS WORK IN YOUR HOME

    THE TIME-LIFE BOOK OF THE FAMILY CAR

    THE TIME-LIFE FAMILY LEGAL GUIDE

    THE TIME-LIFE BOOK OF FAMILY FINANCE

TIME-LIFE LIBRARY OF ART

# Modern American Painting

by the Editors of TIME–LIFE BOOKS

TIME-LIFE BOOKS, Alexandria, Virginia

Time-Life Books Inc.
is a wholly owned subsidiary of
**TIME INCORPORATED**

FOUNDER: Henry R. Luce 1898-1967

*Editor-in-Chief:* Hedley Donovan
*Chairman of the Board:* Andrew Heiskell
*President:* James R. Shepley
*Vice Chairman:* Roy E. Larsen
*Corporate Editor:* Ralph Graves

**TIME-LIFE BOOKS INC.**
MANAGING EDITOR: Jerry Korn
*Executive Editor:* David Maness
*Assistant Managing Editors:* Dale Brown,
Martin Mann
*Art Director:* Tom Suzuki
*Chief of Research:* David L. Harrison
*Director of Photography:* Melvin L. Scott
*Senior Text Editors:* William Frankel,
Diana Hirsh
*Assistant Art Director:* Arnold C. Holeywell

CHAIRMAN: Joan D. Manley
*President:* John D. McSweeney
*Executive Vice Presidents:* Carl G. Jaeger
(U.S. and Canada),
David J. Walsh (International)
*Vice President and Secretary:* Paul R. Stewart
*Treasurer and General Manager:*
John Steven Maxwell
*Business Manager:* Peter G. Barnes
*Sales Director:* John L. Canova
*Public Relations Director:* Nicholas Benton
*Personnel Director:* Beatrice T. Dobie
*Production Director:* Herbert Sorkin
*Consumer Affairs Director:* Carol Flaumenhaft

**TIME-LIFE LIBRARY OF ART**
SERIES EDITOR: Robert Morton
Editorial Staff for
*Modern American Painting:*
*Text Editor:* Jay Brennan
*Picture Editor:* Patricia Maye
*Designer:* Leonard Wolfe
*Staff Writers:* Tony Chiu, Paula Pierce,
Suzanne Seixas, John von Hartz
*Chief Researcher:* Martha T. Goolrick
*Researchers:* Evelyn Constable,
Margo Dryden, Villette Harris
*Art Assistant:* Mervyn Clay

EDITORIAL PRODUCTION
*Production Editor:* Douglas B. Graham
*Operations Manager:* Gennaro C. Esposito
*Assistant Production Editor:*
Feliciano Madrid
*Quality Director:* Robert L. Young
*Assistant Quality Director:* James J. Cox
*Associate:* Serafino J. Cambareri
*Copy Staff:* Susan B. Galloway (chief),
Patricia Miller, Florence Keith,
Celia Beattie
*Picture Department:* Dolores A. Littles,
Elizabeth A. Dagenhardt
*Traffic:* Barbara Buzan

### The Authors

The introductory chapter for this book was written by Dr. John W. McCoubrey, who also served as the consultant. Dr. McCoubrey, a professor in the Department of the History of Art at the University of Pennsylvania, also acted as the consultant for *The World of Turner* in the TIME-LIFE Library of Art and is the author of *American Tradition in Painting.* Chapters I, II and III and their picture essays were written by John von Hartz. The remaining chapters and picture essays were written by Tony Chiu, Paula Pierce, Suzanne Seixas and Robert Morton.

### The Consulting Editor

H. W. Janson is Professor of Fine Arts at New York University, where he is also Chairman of the Department of Fine Arts at Washington Square College. Among Professor Janson's numerous publications are his *History of Art* and *The Sculpture of Donatello.*

### On the Slipcase

A detail from Jasper Johns's *Numbers in Color,* painted in 1958-1959. reveals the artist's preoccupation with the quality and texture of paint and with the iconography of contemporary life. Johns has also created surprising and beautiful paintings using bull's-eye targets, the American flag and maps of the United States, suggesting that even such common images can yield fresh meaning and sensation when treated in unfamiliar ways. He often integrates real fragments of the ephemera of daily living into his paintings; barely visible beneath the lower number seven in this work is a piece of a newspaper cartoon. The full painting is reproduced on page 170.

### End Papers

*Front and Back:* Details from Jackson Pollock's painting *Number 26* (reproduced in full on page 6) show the free-flowing technique of spatters and dribbles that characterize Pollock's inventive style.

CORRESPONDENTS: Elisabeth Kraemer (Bonn); Margot Hapgood, Dorothy Bacon (London); Susan Jonas, Lucy T. Voulgaris (New York); Maria Vincenza Aloisi, Josephine du Brusle (Paris); Ann Natanson (Rome). Valuable assistance was also provided by Carolyn T. Chubet (New York).

# Contents

# What Is
# American Art?

In the first seven decades of the 20th Century, decades of extraordinary invention and change, American art can be said to have come of age. The first significant steps toward that maturity came in the early 1900s, with the advent of a strong, realistic style rooted in a tradition of naturalism that went all the way back to the earliest expressions of America's artists. From these beginnings American painting progressed through a variety of experiments, finally breaking through in the late 1940s with a native style called Abstract Expressionism, a revolutionary approach that put the United States for the first time in the vanguard of art.

To understand this evolution, one must examine it in the light of America's changing nature, and of attitudes toward art in this country and abroad. The history of European painting has always been marked by a formal logic, one development leading to the next. In contrast, American painting, until very recently at least, has been a series of inventions and reactions, fits and starts; it has not known the steady process that only an established tradition of painting can bring. The roots of the 20th Century paintings reproduced in this volume actually lie in different styles ranging through four hundred years of European art. Far from the art capitals of the Old World, our artists have grappled with the look of each new style as it came along. Even those Americans closest to the most recent "isms" abroad—Fauvism, Cubism, Futurism and Surrealism—did not contribute to their births. Consequently their grasp of the formal language of new styles has frequently been unsure. Yet in that very unsureness there has been a freedom to change the accents of each new language and, consciously or not, to develop an American idiom out of it. Again and again these changes have stemmed from attitudes U.S. artists have consistently held about the purposes of their art, the materials of which it was made and the environment in which they worked. In these attitudes, and in the changes they have worked on a variety of borrowed styles, lies the inner coherence of our art and its uniquely American qualities.

Americans have always felt that they had to make their art useful,

7

to put it to work, perhaps because they distrusted it. Rarely have they painted for the sheer joy of painting, or enjoyed painting for its direct sensuous appeal as Europeans have done. To the Puritans, art was a frivolous luxury. In the colonies and the early republic, portraiture was virtually the only type of painting we had, or would permit. And the early portraitists, who perhaps knew their own limitations, made no attempt to imitate the luxurious brushwork of the older European masters. The sober, clear-edged faces painted by John Singleton Copley and his Boston and New York compatriots, slowly and with infinite care, reflect this lingering aversion to luxury.

Landscape painting flourished for three decades before the Civil War, but whatever innocent escape this type of painting offered, its principal justification was a spiritual one. Our 19th Century landscapists rarely permitted "art," in terms of either personal showmanship or traditional composition, to intrude upon their meditative portrayal of American scenery as they found it—that is, as the Creator had left it. Artists and their public saw a wilderness untouched by man, a visible manifestation of God. "We are in Eden," wrote Thomas Cole, the founder of the first American landscape school, and he and his contemporaries used paint to define each tree, leaf and stone, sacrificing detail only to the truthful rendering of light. Rich effects and painter's flourishes were burned away in the intensity of their observation.

In the decades after the Civil War, a growing and industrious America had little time for the cultivation of art. When the new millionaires sought badges of a culture they did not possess, they acquired European old masters or patronized the academicians here and abroad who imitated the old masters. Meanwhile, our greatest painters, Winslow Homer and Thomas Eakins, went about their work untouched and unaided by this new market for artistic pretension. They were committed to portraying the American scene; they believed in the morality of truth, not of "art" or "style." Their seriousness is evident in all they painted. Even figures shown in some trivial activity—boys playing snap-the-whip in a schoolyard, men boating on a river—behave as though they felt the grave purpose the artists had in painting them.

American painting has often expressed the scale and emptiness of the land itself, and the isolation and loneliness it frequently produces in those who live on it. Landscape painters in the United States have seldom settled down to make a small corner of it their own, as the French painters did at Barbizon or at the congenial resorts on the outskirts of Paris. Americans preferred the great reaches of mountain, fields or shoreline touched lightly by human occupation, places where they themselves were transients. They painted these scenes as they found them, without relying on the compositional formulas that order and make habitable the space of traditional landscape paintings. In contrast to European landscape painting, human figures in these American spaces are given no mastery over nature.

In addition to a pervading sense of space, much of American 20th Century painting reveals an aversion to the sensuous and a desire to express in paint the true conditions of American life. In no other country have artists so consistently put art to work for programs and ideologies that were not born of art itself. Much of our painting, therefore, has remained figurative and frankly narrative.

At the turn of the century the key members of a group of realistic painters, called The Eight or the Ash Can School, took their subject matter from the robust vigor of the city. In the decades between the two World Wars, the collapse of Woodrow Wilson's internationalism and the outbreak of the Depression produced a period of introspection. A new group of artists took up the urban subject matter first introduced by The Eight and focused it on social concern and protest, bread lines and strikes.

In seeking a style, all these realistic painters looked to other models. The art of The Eight was a blunt, vigorous reworking of 17th Century European realists like the Dutchman Hals and the Spaniard Velázquez. Some of the socially conscious painters of the 1930s, especially Raphael Soyer and Reginald Marsh, turned to Goya and Daumier, while others, like Ben Shahn and Philip Evergood, painted in an incisive, caricatural style based on an art form designed to reach most people most effectively, the newspaper cartoon. In their desire to demonstrate that life in America was a subject worthy of the grand tradition of Western art, a group of regional painters also borrowed ambitiously: John Steuart Curry and Thomas Hart Benton from the energetic Baroque of Rubens, Grant Wood from the careful precision of the 15th Century Flemish and German masters he admired.

Among the more individualistic of the realists were men like Edward Hopper, who developed a spare, clean-lined style, and later, Andrew Wyeth, who paid meticulous attention to texture and minute detail. In their paintings both men reminded their viewers that in urban and rural America a sense of personal loneliness and isolation survived from the pioneer years. Hopper's work in particular suggested that America's rapid growth and change had denied its inhabitants a deep physical attachment to the land and had given a look of impermanence to what they had built and rebuilt upon it. In America's vast spaces and in its towered, crowded cities, amid the turmoil of accelerating change, its artists have tried over and over to discover who its people are and what the nation has become.

What of those artists who embraced, or tried to embrace, modernism? The travels of American painters to Europe, and the migration of European painters to America, became much more frequent after the turn of the century; but the pace of innovation abroad was so swift that our artists were no more able to make the welter of foreign styles their own than they had been in the leisurely past. The almost overwhelming variety of these styles took the American public by surprise in the famous New York Armory Show of 1913. By far the most lastingly influential of the new movements was Cubism, both in the sharp, flat geometric forms developed by Picasso and Braque in the teens and the mechanistic forms of a separate group of painters for whom Cubism was less a formal exercise than a new language of the technological age. Among the most original European artists was Marcel Duchamp, who, with Francis Picabia, came to New York during World War I. Although their art seemed to mock the plight of modern man among his machines, Duchamp and Picabia found America exhilarating and were convinced that a spare linear style was especially appropriate in this most technologically advanced country. Their message was lost during the years between the wars, but it re-emerged in some of the most inventive American art of the 1960s.

Americans of the 1920s like Charles Demuth and Charles Sheeler found the angular Cubist style well suited to the ready-made geometry of urban and industrial America—the boxlike factories and offices that were the most visible signs of our modernity. Interestingly, this new American Cubism was closely related to the chaste linear style of our early, self-taught painters. This continuity between the old and the new in American painting is especially apparent in the work of Sheeler, who found visual unity among the modern factories, the early American houses and barns, and the Shaker furniture and implements he painted. Stuart Davis, another of the American Cubists, expressed the vitality and energy of American life more abstractly, but he too employed visual fragments, like advertising images and newspaper headlines, drawn from the American scene.

The second impetus from European modernism came, like the first, as the result of a world war. Stimulated by the presence of many leading painters from abroad, including the Surrealists Max Ernst and André Masson, and caught up in the new cultural vitality of their city, a number of New Yorkers created Abstract Expressionism, a wholly new, different kind of art. Despite its debt to European modernists, the new style was, once again, peculiarly American. The New York School, as it has been called, was not strictly a school; its members were united only by shared views about the purpose of painting, and by their search for new meanings. Uncommitted to any single modern style, they were free to blend the formal ideas of Cubism, for example, with the subjective, spontaneous elements of Surrealism. They were called Abstract Expressionists because they sought through abstract, nonobjective forms to express the most fundamental of human experiences.

In rejecting conventional solutions and aiming for more basic goals, the abstractionists had much in common with earlier American artists. Like the untouched scenery our earlier painters faced, but did not alter, their large, empty canvases represented areas of possibility; in many cases the final form each work would take remained in doubt until it was virtually finished. In the unorthodox ways they used paint, Jackson Pollock, Franz Kline and Willem de Kooning revealed the restlessness and anxiety of mid-20th Century America. Pollock dripped pigments in swirling rhythms directly onto the canvas without trying to dictate what final pattern would emerge; in the nature of his method each track was a decision influencing the next one. Kline's dark configurations present powerful intersections of forces, accompanied by a roughness of surface that makes no compromise in appealing to the viewer. De Kooning applied paint in a more richly colored, sensually textured fashion; nevertheless, he preserved marks of spontaneity and indecision by allowing paint to run untended down the surface or by only half concealing false starts. With these techniques, all three painters avoided traditional manifestations of order to stress the risk and unpredictability of life itself.

Yet, for all their abstract techniques these artists did not ignore the visual raw material of their American environment. The size of Pollock's canvases evokes the majestic scale of earlier landscapes; their swirling energy echoes the twisting contours of Benton, with whom he studied. Kline's slashing strokes of black charge out to the edges of his pictures, implying spaces beyond their limits; his shapes evoke the silhouettes of steel skyscrapers, bridges, iron fire escapes. Such references are most specific in de Kooning's paintings, which contain the inescapable trivia of modern life—traces of lettering from signs, movie-poster goddesses, the colors of cheap plastics. His pictures seem like fragments torn from some larger context of disorder.

The flowering of Abstract Expressionism in the 1940s and 1950s was followed by sharp reactions to what was considered its romantic individualism and undisciplined forms. Pop artists returned emphatically to subject matter, which they found in the brash packaging and mass media of our consumer economy—a man-made, omnipresent environment, more demanding in America than anywhere else. Op artists chose to deal chiefly in visual effect and the austere purity of color for its own sake. The restrained use of paint that has characterized so much of our painting persists in Minimal art. The detached, impersonal quality of these styles is reinforced in some instances by allowing the paint to soak into the canvas, leaving only a residue of color; the texture of the painting remains the texture of the cloth itself. By 1970, still other, newer experiments in art were going on.

But despite the variety of styles evolved over the years, there are unique and unifying elements in American painting that have to do with the facts of American life. American painters, living spiritually and physically at the edge of the mainstream of Western art, have consistently adopted only what they have needed to deal with their special circumstances. Again and again they have hesitated to indulge in the luxury of painting, insisting instead that their art should say something about America and themselves. What they chose to paint—first the wide-open spaces, then the man-made environment, often of similar heroic scale, and often as empty and remote—could not be done solely with styles developed elsewhere. Traditionally, art has been a measure of the human will to order and control. But the vastness of America, its variety and the great forces working change upon it have made this function almost irrelevant. American painters have instead attempted to fulfill the conditions the American poet Wallace Stevens described in his *Prelude to Objects:*

. . . *if, without sentiment, he is what he hears*
*And sees and if, without pathos, he feels what he*
*Hears and sees, being nothing otherwise, having*
*Nothing otherwise, he has not to go to the Louvre to behold himself.*

11

# I

# The Ash Can School

The American mood at the turn of the century was one of euphoric optimism. Thousands of newly wealthy industrialists, stock manipulators and merchants had proved that there was indeed gold in the American Dream. The swelling numbers of the middle class luxuriated in freshly gained status and comfort. Industry was booming; foreign markets were expanding; America's possibilities seemed limitless. The vast majority of the nation's citizens confidently believed that every ambitious, hard-working man would soon be living in clover.

The accepted art of the day reflected this dreamworld quality, and there was considerably more dross in it than gold. The majestic land- and seascapes of Winslow Homer and his brilliant contemporaries of the previous generation still won awards and critical acclaim. Popular taste, however, was Victorian and sentimental; a painting that would prompt a merchant to reach for his wallet might show a pretty girl in a Grecian robe offering laurels to a victor. Equally appealing might be a landscape at sunset with gentle cows filing back to the barn.

The custodians and promoters of this popular, unadventurous style were America's art academies, in which aspiring painters received their training, and without whose stamp of approval few artists could make a sale. Among them were the prestigious Pennsylvania Academy of the Fine Arts in Philadelphia, the National Academy of Design in New York, and the Academy of Painting and Drawing in Cincinnati. The exhibitions staged at these academies were stately, dull and sparsely attended, but wealthy, status-conscious patrons purchased only the type of works seen at them. To maintain "standards," the academies rigidly screened all entries in a show beforehand, lest some alien artistic viewpoint slip in. Artists who did not paint in the academic mode had nowhere else to show their work, for private galleries were equally restrictive; usually, the art on the walls was by the same artists who dominated the academy shows. In short, aspiring artists conformed to the standards of the academies or were forced to consign their work to obscurity.

Small wonder that when one group of artists first began to attract at-

The details of everyday life were the concern of the Ash Can School, which set American painting on a new course in the early 1900s. A striking example is John Sloan's study of a woman hanging out her wash from a tenement fire escape. Filling this mundane scene with color and rough-brushed vitality, Sloan allowed little to escape him: the clothespin in the housewife's mouth is as important a part of the picture as the wind-whipped wash on the roof in the background.

John Sloan: *Woman's Work*, 1911 ·

tention with realistic, nonacademic paintings that reflected the changing contemporary American scene, shock waves reverberated through the art Establishment. While the academies dwelt on art based on previous art, these new painters were concerned with art drawn from life. They left the sanctity of the studio and toured the streets and back alleys. They deliberately captured people in unguarded and relaxed moments—hurrying across busy city intersections, sitting alone in bleak apartments, shopping for clothes. For presuming to paint these simple realities of American existence, the new artists were roundly attacked for wallowing in the sordid; common people at their everyday pursuits were considered beneath artistic consideration. Like outlaws, the realists were branded "The Black Gang." In later years critics referred to their collective endeavors as the "Ash Can School." Although ash cans did figure in some of their early paintings of city street life, the term remains as misleading now as it was then. Ash cans were not their concern; people were.

The leader of the realists was Robert Henry Cozad, better known as Robert Henri. Henri was a man whose life went deep to the roots of the 19th Century American experience. He grew up in Nebraska, where his father, John J. Cozad, owned and farmed a substantial tract of land. Life on the plains was one brutal battle after another; the weather was harsh, grasshoppers invaded the fields, the Sioux and the Pawnee raided the farms, and the cowboys of the cattle barons constantly harassed the farmers whose fences were enclosing their grazing lands. Doggedly, the elder Cozad persevered until his luck ran out in 1882, when he shot and killed a cattleman after a fist fight. To avoid prosecution he fled east with his family, first to New York, then to Atlantic City, where he ran a hotel. To protect his father, Robert Henry Cozad took the assumed name of Robert Henri, giving it an American twist by pronouncing it "Hen-rye."

When he was 21 Henri enrolled in the Pennsylvania Academy, where his strong penchant for realistic art was encouraged by his instructor, Thomas Anshutz, a disciple of Thomas Eakins. To modern eyes one of the finest painters of 19th Century America, Eakins was not widely appreciated in his time. His realistic approach to his subject matter—he actually showed *blood* on the hands of surgeons depicted performing operations—made his work seem crude to polite society and the academicians and he therefore never received the honors he deserved. Henri, however, was a devout admirer of Eakins and of the realism he espoused. He left the Academy in 1888 to continue his art studies in Paris, in part because he wished to examine at first hand the work of the great Édouard Manet, whose vigorous, vibrant brand of realism he found equally appealing.

By the time he returned to America from Europe in 1891, Henri had drawn upon these influences to evolve a robust style of his own, producing broadly painted figures outlined by dramatic lighting and intense shading, a style that he employed to depict what concerned him most—scenes of everyday American life. In a studio that he took at 806 Walnut Street, in the heart of downtown Philadelphia, he lost

This group of artists, most of them members of the Ash Can School, gathered at the Philadelphia studio of the painter Charles Grafly in 1892 after attending *Annie Rooneyo*, one of the theatrical spoofs the group loved to put on. It was on this occasion that the leader of the Ash Can School, Robert Henri, first met a man who would become one of the School's finest painters, John Sloan. Henri is at lower left in a stovepipe hat next to the man with a ring in his nose. Sloan is at center rear, his mustachioed face under the muzzle of an old-fashioned pistol held by the man behind him.

no time in communicating his credo to a group of gifted and enterprising artists that included William Glackens, George Luks, John Sloan and Everett Shinn. Because of Henri and the artists who met at his studio, Philadelphia stands as a spiritual home of the Ash Can School. It was there that they began their studies of slum residents, coal miners and assembly-line workers—subjects that the academicians seemed to believe did not exist in contemporary America, or were not worthy of depiction. Every Tuesday evening the artists would assemble at 806 Walnut, and the meetings invariably were dominated by Henri. He had profited greatly from his years in the museums and artists' haunts of Paris. His convictions were deep, his style—in manner as well as art—completely winning. He would pace among his guests, a rangy, commanding figure, persuasively explaining in a soft and gentle voice his views of art and life.

A born teacher, Henri could always inspire his listeners with his carefully formulated observations about style, craft and subject matter. He maintained that anything could be the subject for a painting. "The tramp sits on the edge of the curb," he once said. "He is all huddled up. His body is thick. His underlip hangs. His eyes look fierce. I feel the coarseness of his clothes against his bare legs. He is not beautiful, but he could well be the motive for a great and beautiful work of art. The subject can be as it may, beautiful or ugly. The beauty of a work of art is in the work itself."

Henri's studio served him and his listeners as more than a lecture hall; it was a club as well. On many nights, beer steins made their rounds. Poker games were begun and indoor scrimmages were organized with plates substituting for footballs and pots of spaghetti for goals. Usually these matches dissolved into spaghetti fights that left splatterings of dried strands decorating the walls for years to come.

A slightly more organized form of chaos were the theatricals writ-

Their theatrical productions brought out the ham in the Philadelphia artists. Below, the normally shy and inarticulate William Glackens is shown dressed as a little girl to sing and dance between acts of a play, although he could not carry a tune. John Sloan took the title role in *Twillbe (far right)*, a burlesque of *Trilby*, a best-selling novel by the English artist and author George du Maurier. Trilby was a wistful, sweet French girl who had frequent lapses of virtue as a model in the Paris Latin Quarter. Her feet, du Maurier wrote, were "happy little dimpled arrangements in innocent young pink and white." Sloan played the part with a fake deformed foot, which peeks from under his gown. A ticket Sloan designed for the show *(right)* is executed in the *art-nouveau* style that he used on his job as artist and poster maker for Philadelphia newspapers.

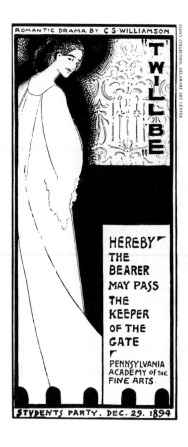

ROMANTIC DRAMA BY C·S·WILLIAMSON

"TWILLBE"

HEREBY THE BEARER MAY PASS THE KEEPER OF THE GATE

PENNSYLVANIA ACADEMY OF THE FINE ARTS.

STUDENTS PARTY. DEC. 29. 1894.

ten and staged by the artists. The productions had such alluring titles as *The Widow Cloonan's Curse* and *The Poisoned Gum-Drop*. One photograph from the time shows Henri and Sloan tied to fake railroad tracks as a cardboard engine bears down on them. Another is of Glackens, generally a painfully shy man, dressed in a little girl's white dress and tiny straw hat and apparently engaged in a song-and-dance routine. One production, a parody of the English artist George du Maurier's novel *Trilby*, featured Shinn in the role of an American expatriate artist named James McNails Whiskers.

Away from the parties, the workday lives of most of the artists were hardly more placid. Glackens, Luks and Shinn were newspaper artist-reporters. Their job was to rush to the scene of an accident, fire or other news event, sketch it and return the drawing to the paper for reproduction in the next edition. In this era of sensational journalism, readers were lured by high-powered circulation wars between papers owned by such giants as Joseph Pulitzer and William Randolph Hearst. Pictures of breaking news events were a sure way to sell newspapers. A quick and efficient way of reproducing photographs had yet to be perfected, but the sketches of fast-working artist-reporters could be transposed to newsprint easily. Thus these men were human cameras serving newspapers the way photographers do today.

Advances in printing and photographic technology drove the artist-reporter out of business by 1900, although he is still used sparingly today to cover stories where cameras are prohibited, as in courts of law. While it existed, however, the job gave the young artists invaluable training in capturing a scene quickly and exactly. To do this they had to develop a fine grasp of detail, a straightforward style and a flair for the dramatics of an event. All these qualities the Philadelphia artist-reporters carried over into their more mature work, the paintings they were to execute in later years.

The undisputed master of the artist-reporter trade was Glackens, whose bright eyes seldom missed a detail. A favorite game of his friends was to ask Glackens to describe a room they had just left. He never forgot a thing, from the molding on the walls to the kind of flowers on the table. For this talent, he was dubbed by his friends "the photographic mind most likely to succeed." His skilled drawings enabled him to move from Philadelphia to Pulitzer's *New York World* and then to *McClure's* magazine, for which he covered the fighting in Cuba during the Spanish-American War.

In Cuba the din of battle did not disturb Glackens as much as a lack of meals. All the other correspondents and artists scrounged enough food from the U.S. Army field kitchens to survive, but the reticent Glackens could not bring himself to do this. As a result, he was usually half-starved. When the legendary Battle of San Juan Hill began, Glackens was an observer. A fellow newsman shouted to him, "Save yourself! We are under fire!" But the artist surprised his friend by barking back, "Beans!"—a plate of which had just been abandoned by a retreating soldier. As the others fled, Glackens dived on the food, raising his head only to call after them, "Cowards!"

The coverage of the war was Glackens' last assignment as an artist-reporter. He became a freelance artist in New York, illustrating books and magazines in a style as fresh and truthful as it had been during his newspaper days. His frank and lifelike drawings of action on the floor of the New York Stock Exchange and of song-pluggers in Tin Pan Alley were a wholesome contrast to the wan, supersophisticated Beautiful People done by the most fashionable illustrator of the day, Charles Dana Gibson, whose sketches of deep-bosomed, wasp-waisted girls came in some eyes to epitomize American beauty. The insipid Gibson girl became as much of an American female symbol as did her male counterpart, the starched Man in the Arrow Shirt.

Glackens supported himself and his family as a commercial artist, but his first love was painting. He devoted every spare moment to canvases depicting vignettes of city life, in which he combined his photographic eye with an exquisite feel for color. In 1912 he was given an opportunity rarely offered an artist; he was sent abroad to purchase paintings for a private collection. His sponsor was Dr. Albert C. Barnes, a man Glackens had grown up with (and played semipro baseball with) in Philadelphia. Barnes had invented a patent medicine he called Argyrol, a preparation that had made him a millionaire. Fortified with $20,000 of Barnes's money, Glackens toured Europe buying the works of such artists as Renoir, Degas, Van Gogh and Cézanne, paintings that in later years would command astronomical prices. These canvases formed the nucleus of the distinguished collection now housed at the Barnes Foundation in Merion, a suburb of Philadelphia.

The most irrepressible and uproarious member of the Ash Can School was George Luks. Life to Luks was a circus in which he acted the role of clown. His clothes were outrageous; he sometimes wore trousers cut off just below the knees, a style he claimed was the rage of the Paris Latin Quarter. His longtime friend Shinn once characterized Luks's clothes as "shadow plaids of huge dimensions, the latest word in suburban realty maps." A consummate mimic, Luks regularly reduced his friends to helpless laughter by jumping up in the middle of a room and faultlessly impersonating everyone present. He also loved to amuse children with an imitation of an entire wedding, starting with the rumbling organ prelude, followed by the minister's solemn intonation, "Augustus Smearcase, do you take this woman . . ."

Luks harbored an abiding fantasy of himself as a prize fighter named "Chicago Whitey," the ferocious winner of at least 150 ring battles. He was such an accomplished actor and talker that many people believed him. A more objective view of Luks's fighting ability was provided by the observant Sloan. "He would often pick a fight in a saloon," Sloan reported, "say something nasty and get things going and then leave the place, with people who had nothing to do with the argument left to finish the fracas." Luks sometimes let his notion of himself as a fighter carry over into his artistic life. He would strike himself on the chest repeatedly while assuring his friends that Frans Hals was inside him trying to fight his way out.

Luks had been reared in the Pennsylvania coal country, the son of a small-town doctor and a mother enamored of art. The children were encouraged to express themselves and Luks and his brother Will did so by forming a vaudeville act. George supplied the clever patter while Will backed him up by playing his guitar. Their stage career proved short-lived; Will was shipped off to medical school (he later became superintendent of a New York clinic) and George embarked for Europe and the life of an artist. For 10 years he led a peripatetic existence, sometimes living with distant relatives (one was a retired lion tamer in Düsseldorf) and frequenting cafés and taverns as much as art classes and museums. On his arrival in Philadelphia he announced that he had been the pupil of many then-prominent European instructors: "Lowenstein, Jensen, Gambrinus and some Frenchmen, from whom I never learned anything, always excepting Renoir, who is great any way you look at him."

Luks served as an artist-reporter in Philadelphia and he too covered the Spanish-American War, for the *Evening Bulletin*. His method of reporting, however, was quite unlike that of Glackens, who spent his days in the field with the troops. Luks tarried in the bars of Havana listening to the war tales of soldiers and other correspondents. He would select a skirmish that sounded exciting, then sketch it, adding graphic captions of his own. The results were as convincing as his acts and impersonations and were greeted with great admiration back in Philadelphia.

Luks eventually moved on to the *New York World*, where he worked with Glackens and Shinn. Not long before, Pulitzer had introduced the first comic strips into his paper as part of his battle to win readers. The prize attraction of "the funnies" was a strip featuring the adventures of a group of urchins, one of them a youngster called "The

Yellow Kid" because he always wore a long yellow nightshirt. When the artist who developed "The Yellow Kid" was lured to Hearst's *New York Journal,* Luks was asked to continue the strip for the *World.* He did so with enormous success and for years the rival papers each carried its own version of "The Yellow Kid."

While supporting himself comfortably on his cartooning, Luks continued his interest in serious painting, prowling the streets and, on occasion, the countryside, in search of arresting human scenes. The sketches and paintings resulting from these forays reveal a wide range of subject matter—longshoremen working on snow-encrusted piers, a polo match on a Long Island estate, poor children playing games or dancing in the street. He once commented in the blunt manner he adopted when speaking of art, "A child of the slums will make a better painting than a drawing-room lady gone over by a beauty shop."

Luks's ebullience, which had animated his whole life, eventually led to his death. In 1933, when he was 66, his body was found one morning in the doorway of a building next to the Sixth Avenue elevated railway in Manhattan. The romanticized stories printed in the newspapers stated that Luks had gone to the shabby section of the city to paint the light of dawn as it filtered down through the tracks, and was set upon by derelicts. What actually happened was quite different. Luks had slipped into a speak-easy and after a few drinks had begun one of his wild routines. One of the other patrons, infuriated by the act, took the artist outside and beat him to death.

In behavior and temperament, John Sloan was the complete opposite of Luks. A judicious man who carefully weighed his every action, he was the last of the artist-reporters to leave Philadelphia for New York. Once there, he spent many hours at the rear window of his studio on West 23rd Street, sketching his neighbors. The paintings from these vigils are vigorous and lively, yet marked by the haunting sense of loneliness that underlies much of big-city life. In his old age Sloan said, "You young people don't realize how sweet—sweet and sad —New York was before Prohibition. But now, who'd want to paint a street strewn with automobiles? The skyline? It's like a comb in the

George Luks loved to act out his fantasies. Here he poses as a great fighter, stripped to the waist *(left)* and pretending to box an unidentified friend. The mock match was staged for a photographer at the Walnut Street studio of Robert Henri. The spectators standing at the left are the artists James Preston, John Sloan and Everett Shinn.

restroom of a filling station. A tooth here and there missing, and all filled with dirt. Unfortunately, we're the dirt."

The struggle of the Ash Can artists for recognition was not without victories. Many of the painters gained reputations among perceptive critics, particularly in New York, where Henri in 1904 established a school on Broadway near what is now the site of Lincoln Center. At it gathered the other members of the old Philadelphia crowd who had moved to New York, as well as such newcomers as George Bellows, Glenn Coleman and Reginald Marsh, who formed the second generation of the realist school.

More important, Henri was named to the New York National Academy of Design in 1906. He had won a prize in 1905 from the Art Institute of Chicago for a portrait called *Lady in Black*, and he had served on the awards jury for the Carnegie International Exhibition that same year. His presence probably accounted for the honorable-mention awards won at the show by Sloan for *The Coffee Line* and by Glackens for his masterpiece, *Chez Mouquin (page 25)*.

Despite their acceptance of Henri, the academies remained essentially hostile to the new realism, throwing only a few minor prizes to other members of the Ash Can School. For his part, Henri did not allow the accolades to deflect him from seeking full recognition for the movement and his fellow artists. He, Sloan and Glackens decided to strike out by staging a show of their own. They enlisted the support of Shinn and Luks, and then were joined by two kindred spirits, Ernest Lawson and Arthur B. Davies. Another artist whose work they all admired, Maurice Prendergast, was invited to contribute from Boston. Each man chipped in $50 to rent the New York gallery of William Macbeth, one of the few dealers in America willing to display art that was not in the academic mold.

The show, which opened on February 3, 1908, indisputably proved that public taste had surpassed that of the academies. From the first moment that the doors of the Macbeth Gallery opened, crowds poured in. At one time there were so many people clamoring for admission that the police were summoned to maintain order. Some of the art critics maintained their customary air of disdain for the work, but many were understanding. Equally incredible to the artists was that nearly $4,000 worth of paintings were sold.

Overnight "The Eight," as the artists represented were dubbed, became the most energetic force in American art. But they did not cling together to husband their newly found fame. As they had in the past, they followed their own courses, painting what they wanted and encouraging other artists to do the same. In 1910, as a result of their efforts, a major show of independent work was mounted in New York. Anyone who wished could enter; there was no jury to judge whether a canvas was worthy of admission. The paintings were hung alphabetically and the hated academic system of awarding prizes was abolished. This show too was a great success. The battle waged by Henri and the Ash Can School had been largely won, and a viable school of art inspired by life had asserted itself in America.

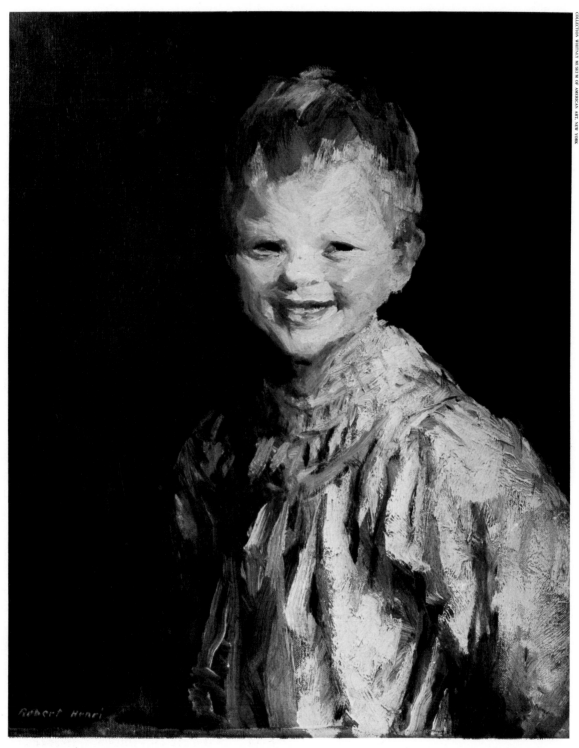

Robert Henri: *Laughing Child,* 1907

# Life in the City

Underlying their various personal styles, the painters of the Ash Can School brought to their work a common zest for humanity that was eloquently preached by their spiritual leader, Robert Henri. Henri's own portraits, like *Laughing Child (above),* fairly brim over with the artist's liking for people —and his work. One of Henri's entries in the landmark 1908 show of "The Eight," *Laughing Child* was hung at the gallery's door, its fresh style indicating that new views of America waited inside.

Everett Shinn: *A Winter's Night on Broadway*, 1899

While other Ash Can artists were extolling the commonplace, Everett Shinn turned his eye for realism on the fashionable world of uptown Manhattan. An artist-reporter and cartoonist, Shinn had come from Philadelphia to work on the *New York World*. But his dream was to place an illustration in the center spread of *Harper's Weekly*, one of the nation's leading periodicals and widely read by the city's elite. His constant badgering finally won him an audience with the editor and publisher of *Harper's*, who told Shinn he was looking for a color drawing showing the Metropolitan Opera House at Broadway and 40th Street in a snowstorm, and asked whether he had ever treated the subject. Shinn looked out the window at a December snowfall and quickly replied that he had just such a drawing at home. He was requested to show it the following morning. He hurried out, bought a cheap box of pastels, and went to the Opera House to sketch. After working all night in his studio, Shinn emerged with the finished pastel *(left)*, which shows well-dressed passengers alighting from hansom cabs and making their way through the storm to the Opera House *(left background)*.

*Harper's* bought the drawing and ran it in the coveted center spread. As he had hoped, the publicity soon netted Shinn commissions as a fashionable painter, an occupation he unabashedly defended to his artist friends. "I was often accused of being a social snob," he said later in life. "Not at all—it's just that the uptown life with all its glitter was more good-looking. . . . Ah, the clothes then —the movement, the satins, women's skirts and men's coats and the sweep of furs and swish of wild boas, oh Lord!"

Robert Henri: *Portrait of William Glackens*, 1904

The influence of the French Impressionist Édouard Manet left its mark on many paintings by the realists. Henri made no attempt to disguise his indebtedness in the full-length portrait of his friend and fellow artist William Glackens *(left)*. In its pose and lack of formal, detailed background, it bears a marked resemblance to a number of portraits by the French master. Glackens, who learned painting from Henri, continued the homage to Manet in his best-known work, *Chez Mouquin (right)*. In its setting, a fashionable New York restaurant, in its mirrored images and in its piquant delineation of character, the painting strikingly recalls Manet's *Bar at the Folies-Bergère*. The mustachioed man holding the glass is James B. Moore, an art patron and bon vivant. Moore is accompanied by one of his many lady friends, whom he referred to as his "daughters." Shown in the mirror between the couple is a rear view of Glackens' wife; the art critic Charles FitzGerald is reflected at the right.

William Glackens: *Chez Mouquin*, 1905

William Glackens: *The Shoppers*, 1908

William Glackens: *Portrait of the Artist's Wife*, 1905

Glackens was a born illustrator but oil painting was difficult for him. He spent long and tedious hours at his easel; the resulting canvases nevertheless conveyed a magical air of spontaneity. Moreover, his gift for characterization never deserted him. In the portrait of his wife *(above)*, done the year after they were married, he catches deftly the sly wit and genteel manner that marked her personality. In *The Shoppers (left)*, Mrs. Glackens and Mrs. Everett Shinn, at right, casually examine dresses. Shown at the 1908 exhibition of "The Eight," this painting was considered vulgar by viewers accustomed to idealized portraits of ladies at their formal best.

John Sloan's enthusiasm for the everyday events of Manhattan infected his work. To him, a group of young women drying their hair on a rooftop radiated such delight that the act transcended its humble surroundings. Free from the cramped confines of stuffy apartments, Sloan's subjects seem to expand in the sunlight as they let down their hair and bask in the warmth while a line of laundry flaps in the background. It is a scene that no academic painter would have deemed worthy of his time, yet it is as full of unexpected pleasures as is the city itself. This sunny canvas was entered in the Armory Show of 1913, where Theodore Roosevelt himself praised it. Sloan's bad luck in selling his work persisted, however; neither the former President nor anyone else bought it.

Sloan did not sell his first painting until he was past 40. He made his living as an art teacher, using every spare moment to patrol the city, searching for subject matter. During these tours he became so wrapped up in the city's people and problems that he ran for the state assembly as a Socialist in 1908. He was defeated, much to his relief; painting, not politics, was his business. When a friend asked him why he kept on in the face of so few sales, he replied, "The only reason I am in the profession is because it is fun."

John Sloan: *Sunday, Girls Drying Their Hair*, 1912

George Bellows: *Stag at Sharkey's*, 1907

Two boxers go at it hot and heavy on a stag night at Tom Sharkey's Athletic Club in New York City in this masterpiece of American sports painting by George Bellows. The canvas is actually more than a sports vignette; it is a landmark of realism as Bellows sets the tension of the straining boxers against the rows of cigar-smoking men passively awaiting first blood—or a knockout.

A topflight athlete himself, Bellows supported himself in New York by playing semipro baseball on weekends. This predilection for sports lured him to Sharkey's club, which was near Robert Henri's art school on upper Broadway, at which Bellows was the prize student. A clear-eyed, affirmative man, Bellows had a natural self-confidence that glows in his work. His enthusiasm for art—and life—made him a natural ally for Henri. Somewhat younger than the other Ash Can artists, he profited from the acceptance they won for their art. In 1908, at 26, he was named an associate of the conservative National Academy of Design, the youngest man ever elected—a distinct honor for a realist painter.

Paintings like *Stag at Sharkey's* made Bellows a celebrity, but his work was not confined to sports. His landscapes surpassed in power and range the best works of the artists of the 19th Century Hudson River School and his portraits are among the finest done by an American in this century. His casual scenes of people at leisure shine with the effortless grace that dignifies all his work. His paintings grew in maturity as he aged, but his career was tragically cut short when he died in 1925 at 42 of a ruptured appendix.

George Luks: *The Old Duchess,* 1905

Georges Luks, a lovable carouser, spent much of his time reeling around the gamy Lower East Side of Manhattan, drinking, talking and watching. Back at his studio he turned out paintings at a furious rate, producing six of his best during the year 1905 alone. Among these was a portrait of a red-nosed slattern he titled *The Old Duchess (above)*; another was *The Spielers (right)*, an engaging study of two slum girls in a carefree dance. Still another Luks work from 1905 was *Hester Street (overleaf)*, a tribute to one of the busiest marketplaces on the Lower East Side. With John Sloan's *Election Night* and *Fifth Avenue*, also shown on the following pages, *Hester Street* illumines the ability of the Ash Can School to create bright tableaux of American life. The desire of all the Ash Can artists to put real experience on canvas was sung out by Luks himself when he cried, "Guts! Guts! Life! Life! That's *my* technique!"

George Luks: *The Spielers*, 1905

George Luks: *Hester Street*, 1905

John Sloan: *Election Night in Herald Square*, 1907

John Sloan: *Fifth Avenue*, 1909

35

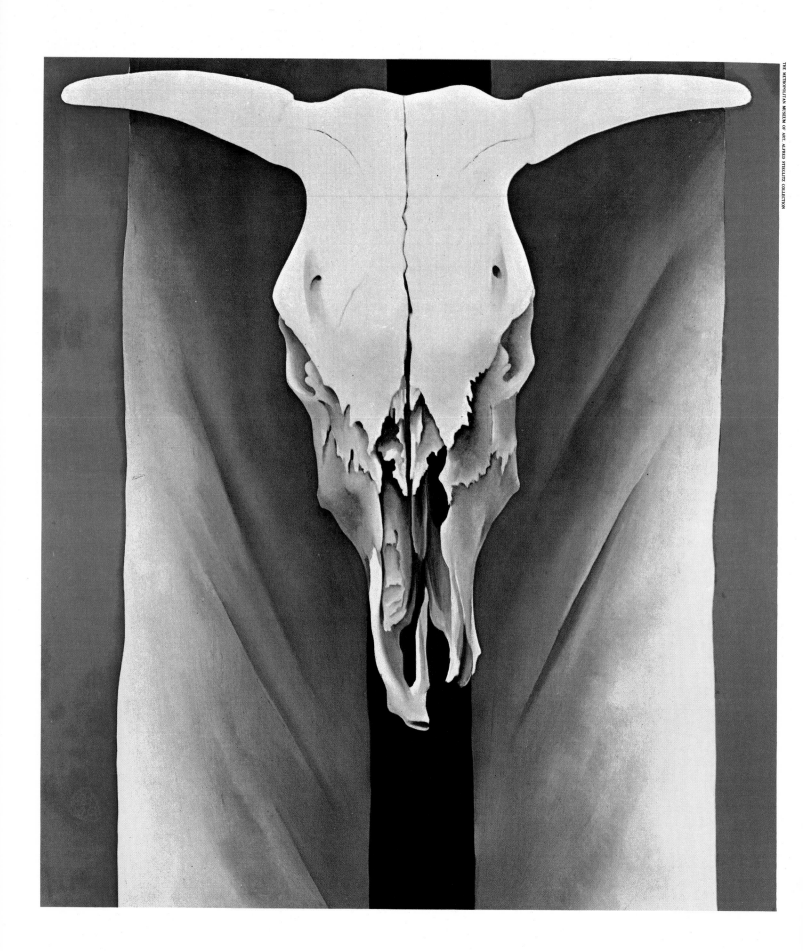

# II

# The Impact
# of Abstraction

The application of abstract concepts to American themes is illustrated in a stunning painting by Georgia O'Keeffe. While living in New Mexico, she became intrigued by the sun-bleached bones of dead cattle strewn across the desert. In this picture, part of a series of highly personal abstract works, she used the stark shape of a skull to convey the barren, harsh beauty of the American Southwest.

Georgia O'Keeffe: *Cow's Skull: Red, White and Blue*, 1931-1936

As the Ash Can School struggled for recognition, a different group of American painters was waging another battle to cast off tradition and establish even more radical approaches to art. These artists—Stuart Davis, Max Weber, John Marin, Arthur Dove, Marsden Hartley, Georgia O'Keeffe and a handful of others—represented the first wave of abstractionism in the United States. They were a dedicated band, and had to be. Their work, inspired by European pioneers like Matisse and Picasso and ranging across a gamut of substyles from Synchromism to Futurism, was subjected to massive public and critical ridicule. Nevertheless, they opened a path that enabled artists of a later generation to create increasingly original varieties of abstractionism.

One major reason for the difficulties encountered by the early abstractionists is that "abstract" art, by its very nature, eludes not only easy comprehension but easy definition. Most of its practitioners, indeed, deplore the term, but it has become a useful, almost unavoidable, convention. Quite simply, abstractionism denotes any art that does not present the world in straightforward, representational form. The abstract artist, as contrasted with the strictly representational one, feels free literally to abstract ideas or shapes from his surroundings, or from his own thoughts, and arrange them as he sees fit to achieve the effect he wants.

Aside from problems of definition and acceptance, the first American abstractionists began with another basic disadvantage. Abstract art was born and raised in Europe, not America. Its progenitors had their roots deep in the revolution that took place in European art in the latter half of the 19th Century. Manet and the Impressionists had first shocked Paris with nontraditional subject matter drawn from everyday life, and light-struck evocations of color done with dash, wit and charm. They were followed by Cézanne, Van Gogh and Gauguin, who turned the Renaissance canons of painting upside down with geometric refinements of natural form and bold, unreal colors that charged their art with emotion.

Nor had the revolution abated after the turn of the century. In 1905

Matisse and the Fauves, the "wild beasts" who used vibrant, expressive color, staged their first show, at the Salon d'Automne in Paris. Then, in 1908, Picasso and Braque unveiled Cubism in Paris. This daring new style, carrying Cézanne's ideas still further, left even the most sympathetic viewers of avant-garde art dumb-struck. Cubism was the artistic revolution gone mad, forms dissected into geometrical patterns and then arbitrarily reassembled into interlocking planes of no discernible relationship. There was beauty in the flat patterns of Cubism, but few saw it.

For more than half a century, the general European public had reeled under the bombardment of a bewildering variety of art exercises. But more astute artists and connoisseurs in Europe and the United States saw that in them lay the way of the future. Abstraction was a natural evolution; it would finally liberate artists from the chains of tradition and lift art to hitherto-unrealized heights. To avant-garde American artists Europe was the only place where the mysteries of modern art could be unraveled.

Accordingly, between 1900 and the outbreak of World War I, in 1914, many American artists made obligatory pilgrimages to Paris. In 1908 there were enough of them in the city to form a New Society of American Artists, the revitalization of a more conservative group organized some years earlier. In Europe the possibilities of the new art forms seemed endless, and the Americans unabashedly experimented with all of them in their own work. But when these artists returned to America, their new styles made them aliens in a hostile land.

In all of America there was but one sanctuary for them, the New York studio-showroom of the master photographer Alfred Stieglitz. A blunt, fastidious, opinionated and frequently gloomy man, Stieglitz was a seer in both photography and painting. Almost singlehandedly he transformed the simple act of picture taking into an art form. His limitless patience in waiting for the exact moment to shoot a picture, his extraordinary grasp of the mechanics of camera, film and darkroom, and his belief that photography could be an independent art with its own esthetic established him as a giant in his field.

Stieglitz early recognized the nature of the European art revolution. Like the American abstract painters, he made frequent journeys to Europe, traveling there four times between 1904 and 1911. In large part these voyages were undertaken to allow him to escape what he regarded as the numbing Philistine climate of America. While in Paris, he was often escorted through the studios of the most advanced painters and sculptors. His guide was Max Weber, an American artist who had been a student of Matisse and whose happy acceptance of the new art forms was reflected in his lively and daring work *Interior with Still Life (page 53)*. Like other expatriate Americans, he tried everything, a habit that prompted a critic to say of one of Weber's shows, "All the moderns seem to be here, but where are the Webers?"

In New York Stieglitz once contended that his goal was "to establish for myself an America in which I could breathe as a free man." It was toward this end that he and the young painter and photographer

Edward Steichen in 1905 had founded the Little Gallery of the Photo-Secession at 291 Fifth Avenue—a rented brownstone that came to be known in the art world as "291." The name Photo-Secession was Stieglitz' idea, which he defined simply as "seceding from the accepted idea of what constitutes a photograph." Later he applied the same criterion to the paintings and sculpture he showed at his studio, invariably choosing whatever "seceded" from accepted ways.

The "291" studio was inelegant, cramped and crowded, but at various times it displayed a stunning range of modern European work. Stieglitz showed for the first time in America the watercolors of Cézanne, Picasso and Rodin, the sculpture of Matisse and Brancusi, the oils of Rousseau. He also mounted the first exhibitions of the American abstractionists: Hartley, Maurer, Marin, Dove, as well as Arthur B. Carles, Stanton Macdonald-Wright and Weber.

One of the artists Stieglitz discovered was Georgia O'Keeffe. From the beginning, he was enchanted by her work. On first viewing a collection of her abstract drawings shown him by a mutual friend, he exclaimed: "Finally, a woman on paper!" From her exhibits at "291" Georgia O'Keeffe gained a measure of fame, primarily for her lush studies of flowers, many of which she painted in extreme close-up detail. She and Stieglitz, who was 23 years her senior, developed a deep mutual respect that eventually blossomed into matrimony. She was a favorite model for Stieglitz, the subject of some 500 of his photographic portraits and studies.

Miss O'Keeffe, who preferred to be called by her maiden name even after her marriage, recalled in 1968 the days at the Stieglitz studio. "At first the men didn't want me around. They couldn't take a woman artist seriously. I would listen to them talk and I thought, my, they are dreamy. I felt much more prosaic but I knew I could paint as well as some of them who were sitting around talking. But I was very fond of [the American abstractionist] Charles Demuth. He was amusing, very elegant, though he had a club foot and diabetes. When he came to town he'd eat things he shouldn't, so he'd stay till he got sick, then go home. Demuth and I always talked about doing a big picture together, all flowers. I was going to do the tall things up high, he was going to do the little things below." They never did execute the project, but Demuth attained a reputation of his own with such exuberant works as *I Saw the Figure 5 in Gold (page 56)*, a meticulously rendered abstraction inspired by a line from a poem by William Carlos Williams.

**M**iss O'Keeffe was saddled with much of the mundane work around the "291" studio, framing pictures and hanging paintings for forthcoming exhibitions. Not only that, she had to care for Stieglitz, a considerable job in itself. "Alfred always insisted on wearing a certain kind of tie, a particular type of sock and underwear and shirt. I used to have to walk all over town trying to find those special kinds. Stieglitz was a funny man—he was pretty special though. He was one of those people who enjoyed his gloom, but you could make him laugh about it. He ate almost nothing and all the wrong things. He lived on energy, on interest. I've listened to him in intense debate with someone and wound up feeling as if I'd been beaten about the body with sandbags."

To break the routine, Miss O'Keeffe in 1929 began retreating to New Mexico in the summers. After Stieglitz died in 1946, she moved to that austere land, whose spare, stark qualities she employed in many of her later paintings *(page 36)*. Like Miss O'Keeffe, several of the American abstractionists withdrew to the countryside where they found renewed inspiration in nature. Marin and Hartley did much of their best work in Maine and Dove settled in Connecticut.

For all his advocacy of modern painters, Stieglitz was not an agent; he rejected the idea of profit from art and seemed genuinely embarrassed by talk of material things. He existed for much of his life on stipends from his father, a wealthy wool merchant, and on gifts and loans from friends. His object at "291" was not to discover artists whose work would elicit high fees with proper time and recognition. He wanted rather to provide an atmosphere of creative freedom, a world set apart from the commonplace struggle for existence. Nor did he hide the influence that the modern painters had on his own work. His photographs often reflected the experimental modes of abstractions, similarly capturing the beauty of form and mood.

Stieglitz and the American abstractionists who gathered around him were constantly badgered by a bewildered public to explain what their art represented. Their definitions are among the simplest and most direct in the often tangled jargon of modern art. Essentially they declared that a painting must be judged for itself alone. It must not be compared to anything in the real world. A painting was an original, independent object of art from which the viewer could derive whatever he wished.

Each painter tried repeatedly to convey this message. Marin urged: "Don't everlastingly read messages into paintings. There's the Daisy. You don't rave over or read messages into it; you just look at that bully little flower. Isn't that enough!" Stieglitz, too, showed a thinly

Georgia O'Keeffe standing in front of one of her huge studies of flowers indicates their remarkable size. Since Miss O'Keeffe was married to photographer Alfred Stieglitz, it had been assumed that her inspiration for these giant paintings was the photographic enlargement of close-up details. But the artist recently said that photography had no influence on her flower paintings. When she started doing them in the 1920s, she was fascinated by the skyscrapers being built all around her in New York City. She decided to make her flowers "big like the huge buildings going up. People will be startled: they'll *have* to look —and they did."

veiled impatience with those who asked him to interpret modern art. "You will find as you go through life," he once said, "that if you ask what a thing means, a picture, or music, or whatever, you may learn something about the people you ask, but as for learning about the thing you seek to know, you will have to sense it in the end through your own experience, so that you had better save your energy and not go through the world asking what cannot be communicated in words. If the artist could describe in words what he does, then he would never have created it."

This elevation of the artist's personal vision over the public's demand for the representational and the recognizable was difficult for most viewers, and many artists, to accept. Even Robert Henri, the crusader for fresh approaches in American art, shied away from the abstractionists. Henri, the artist from the frontier country, was profoundly committed to what is sometimes called democracy in art; he championed populist paintings that would speak to the multitudes across the huge continent. Henri believed that abstract art was intellectual and esoteric, done for the enjoyment and appreciation of the select few. In time he learned to acknowledge the skill of the modern masters, but he remained convinced that the range of abstractionism was too narrow for Americans.

Stieglitz, in all fairness, had never pretended to advocate a democratic or populist art. He and the moderns believed in art purely for its own sake. Their work was for the appreciation of the enlightened and receptive, no matter how few in number they might be.

While the two schools shared the common goal of breaking the academic grip on American art, the gap between them continued to widen. Stieglitz was annoyed when the realists staged an independent show in 1910, not so much because of scorn for their work, but because he felt that the exhibition took attention away from his own displays of modern works at "291." Before long, Henri and Stieglitz took to ignoring each other in public.

To many artists—realists, moderns and academicians alike—the squabbling among factions seemed a disservice not only to art itself but to the American public. The stern façade of the academies had been shaken by the success of the Ash Can School and to a lesser extent by the interest among the avant-garde in the shows at "291." Many artists felt that the time had come to band together to save American art from internecine warfare.

Consequently, members of the three schools formed the Association of American Painters and Sculptors in 1911. The Association's first project was to mount a comprehensive exhibition that would show the public the broad spectrum of contemporary American art. The end result of this effort was the New York Armory Show of 1913, the most significant, improbable and iconoclastic art exhibit ever presented in America. Ironically, this precedent-shattering show was conceived and planned by moderate academicians and realists whose views ran from conservative to mildly progressive. None of the founders had envisioned, or desired, a controversial show that would throw American art into turmoil and provide the viewing public with enough ammunition to fire at practicing artists for decades to come. Yet that is exactly what they got.

The Association decided, democratically, that the proposed show would represent all the current American schools, including the abstractionist. But finding a man to serve as organizer proved almost impossible; no artist was available who could communicate easily with the realists, academicians and abstractionists alike. The wounds inflicted by years of feuding were still fresh, and the show threatened to founder before it was even launched. Then it occurred to someone to approach Arthur B. Davies.

Davies was an artist whose fantasy paintings, often depicting wraithlike women in mythical settings, neither offended nor excited anyone in the various schools—and thus he was acceptable to all sides. He had been an original member of "The Eight," whose show in 1908 had presaged the rise of realism, and he was the only member of that group to make regular visits to the Stieglitz studio. Little was known of him personally; his private life was as enigmatic as his painting. There was good reason for this, as it turned out. Davies was a freethinker and had a family by each of two wives. He was to reveal another of his secret passions—for modern European art—after he took command of the Armory Show.

Davies suggested that the show include at least some painters from the European modern movements. The members of the Association somewhat reluctantly agreed. They wanted to please Davies, little suspecting what he had in mind. Almost immediately Davies and the painter Walt Kuhn, who had been chosen secretary of the Association, laid plans for transforming the exhibition into a glittering showcase for the talented European moderns. Both men had become convinced through trips abroad that this was the art Americans should be shown.

To encourage Europe's finest painters to enter, Davies and Kuhn toured the Continent in 1912. They visited artists in their studios, selling them on the proposed show. They fell again under the magical spell of Matisse and contracted to bring as much of his work as they could to New York. In all, the trip intoxicated them. They were certain that the genius of the European moderns would be greeted with genuine enthusiasm in America. "We want this old show of ours to mark the starting point of the new spirit in art," Kuhn wrote ecstatically. "I feel it will show its effects even further and make the big wheel turn over in both hemispheres."

They had every reason to believe that America was ready for an infusion of new styles. The United States was then gripped by a compulsion for change and reform. The economic panic of 1907 had been severe enough to raise serious doubts about blind reliance on big-business monopolies; court dockets were crowded with cases brought under the Sherman Antitrust Act. In 1912 Theodore Roosevelt's progressive Bull Moose Party split from the conservative Republican Party that had nominated William Howard Taft for a second term and took enough votes from him to cause the election of the reform Democrat Woodrow Wilson. Armies of women were marching and demonstrating for equality, demanding, among other things, the right to vote, which they eventually won in 1919.

Intellectual circles shared the quest for the new. Pioneering "little" magazines like *Dial, The New Republic* and Stieglitz' own *Camera Work* featured articles by proponents of "modernism." Modern painting, through its bold directions, came to symbolize the utopian spirit of these articles. As one observer wrote of modern art, "It shakes the old foundations and leads to a new life, whether the programs and ideas have permanent validity or not."

In this optimistic mood the entries to the show, more than 1,600 in all, were gathered at the 69th Regiment Armory on Lexington Avenue in New York. The works were grouped according to the nationalities of the artists. The paintings were hung on partitions covered with burlap, sculptures dotted the floor, and overhead were draped garlands of evergreens donated by Gertrude Vanderbilt Whitney, herself a sculptor of some talent.

If any of the members of the Association had been uneasy over the passion of Davies and Kuhn for European art, they now found their apprehensions fully justified. On a February night in 1913, just before

This menu, signed by the guests, is a souvenir of the dinner given for art critics by the artists who sponsored the 1913 Armory Show. The dinner was something of a surprise—most of the critics had been confused or angered by the work at the show. But the artists tried to win them over with fraternal humor, dedicating the occasion "To our friends and enemies of the press." The reproduction on the menu of Marcel Duchamp's controversial *Nude Descending a Staircase*, however, reminded the critics of the type of art championed by the American artists. Even in the friendly atmosphere the critics could not hide their displeasure with the exhibition. One warned, "It was a good show, but don't do it again."

the show was to open, Henri, a lean man in his late forties, wandered around the floor of the Armory. At the French section he stopped and stared. Before him was a breathtaking array of the modern masters —paintings and sculptures by Matisse, Picasso, Cézanne, Van Gogh, Léger, Dufy. In their midst was that audacious masterpiece, *Nude Descending a Staircase* by Marcel Duchamp, an artist who was then only 25. Henri was stunned by the spectacle.

By chance, Davies and Walter Pach, a former student of Henri but now a prominent abstract artist and critic, approached him. The believers in modernism were face to face with the standard-bearer of American realism and democratic art. After a few halting exchanges, Henri turned to Pach and said, "I hope that for every French picture that is sold, you sell an American one."

"That's not the proportion of merit," Pach said of Henri's one-to-one remark, meaning that sales had nothing whatsoever to do with real artistic achievement. Henri responded slowly, "If the Americans find they've just been working for the French, they won't be prompted to do this again."

Henri's forebodings proved correct. The foreign entries sold briskly; some $30,000 worth of them were purchased. American work moved only moderately well, to the tune of $13,600. And Henri was right on his second count too: there was never to be another eclectic exhibition on the scale of the Armory Show, combining the works of all the American schools. Instead of bridging the gaps between academicians, realists and abstractionists, the Association and its show had succeeded only in driving the schools farther apart. There was, however, one major benefit: the Armory Show established abstractionism as a powerful and exciting force in American art.

But not immediately, and by no means easily. Some perceptive critics were ecstatic over the show, but the public greeted it with a mixture of jocularity and outrage. Even the relatively sophisticated *Art News* was exasperated. It ran a contest inviting its readers to find the nude in *Nude Descending a Staircase*. The winner advanced the notion that the nude was a male, a claim an impartial observer might still have difficulty disproving. Theodore Roosevelt decided in an article that the painting reminded him of a Navajo blanket. It was also characterized as a "staircase descending a nude." Columnists, cartoonists and anonymous creators of doggerel found easy exercises for their wit with Cubism, Futurism and Duchamp. The laughter and catcalls would accompany abstract art throughout most of its history in America.

The startling public reaction to modern art was dismissed by its supporters as an expression of massive ignorance. What the American artists found personally shocking was the discovery that they were far behind the Europeans. They knew that from then on whatever they tried in abstractionism would be measured against the masterful European entries displayed at the Armory Show. It was a challenge they did not take lightly. They had learned the concepts from the Europeans, but in the future their vitality and originality would stamp their works as indisputably American.

Stanton Macdonald-Wright: *Abstraction on Spectrum (Organization, 5)*, c. 1915

# An American Avant-Garde

The early American abstractionists, following the lead of their European counterparts, experimented with a dazzling variety of styles inspired by everything from plant forms to machines. One of the first genuine innovations by American painters was Synchromism (literally, "with color"), which relied on color alone to provide both form and content. The new style produced vibrant harmonies in colored circles and curves, as seen in this work by Stanton Macdonald-Wright, one of the founders of the movement.

COLLECTION WHITNEY MUSEUM OF AMERICAN ART, NEW YORK

Marsden Hartley: *Painting, Number 5*, 1914-1915

The militaristic mood of Germany before World War I is caught by Marsden Hartley in this work incorporating military emblems and decorations like the Iron Cross and painted in the Imperial colors —black, white and red. In typical abstractionist manner, however, the artist titled the work simply *Painting, Number 5*. A rugged New Englander, Hartley spent some time in Berlin working in the mode of the German Expressionists, whose bright, raw colors and nontraditional designs horrified the conservative

46

Joseph Stella: *Battle of Light, Coney Island,* 1914

German art world. Returning to America, Hartley in time abandoned this style and painted roughhewn views of the people and landscape of his native Maine.

Joseph Stella's riotous study of a famous amusement park at night *(above)* reveals the artist's infatuation with Italian Futurism, a style of painting objects as they might look while in motion. Stella's kinetic, sometimes kaleidoscopic, abstractions managed to convey in a fresh way the tumult and excitement of 20th Century American life.

47

Born in France, Cubism took different directions in the hands of American abstractionists. In *Lower Manhattan (below)*, one of his many Cubistic watercolors of the city, John Marin favored soft lines, breaking the buildings down into planes and angles but rounding their edges. In addition, he made the tone of the work light and airy, leaving areas of the surface bare. A folksy Yankee who used such rustic phrases as "humdinger" and "crackerjack," Marin had an almost mystical appreciation for New York: "I see great forces at work, great movements, the large buildings and the small buildings, the warring of the great and small. . . . While these powers are at work . . . I can hear the sound of their strife, and there is a great music being played."

Such poetic flights aside, Marin was a disciplined perfectionist as an artist, and a master of understatement. He once compared his work to a golf game—the fewer strokes the better. He was also concerned with the layout of the course, often turning his paintings upside down and sideways to judge balance and composition.

The variety of Cubism practiced by Lyonel Feininger was by comparison hard-edged and crisp. His *Gelmeroda, VIII (right)*, one of a series of paintings titled after a town in Germany, shows a cool authority, a demonstration of his belief that the "whole world is nothing but order."

John Marin: *Lower Manhattan*, 1922

Lyonel Feininger: *Gelmeroda, VIII*, 1921

49

The Rope Dancer Accompanies Herself With Her Shadows

Man Ray: *The Rope Dancer Accompanies Herself with Her Shadows*, 1916

Early abstract art in America was not without its humorous side. Man Ray's *The Rope Dancer Accompanies Herself with Her Shadows (above)* is a bright, sardonic jest that mocks the strict representationalism of academic art in sophisticated Cubist style. In its suggestion that the world is but a reflection of reality, *Rope Dancer* epitomizes Dadaism, a style transported to New York City by Marcel Duchamp and Francis Picabia when they fled Europe and World War I. A nihilistic intellectual revolt against war, materialism and virtually all art, modern and traditional, Dadaism held that human progress

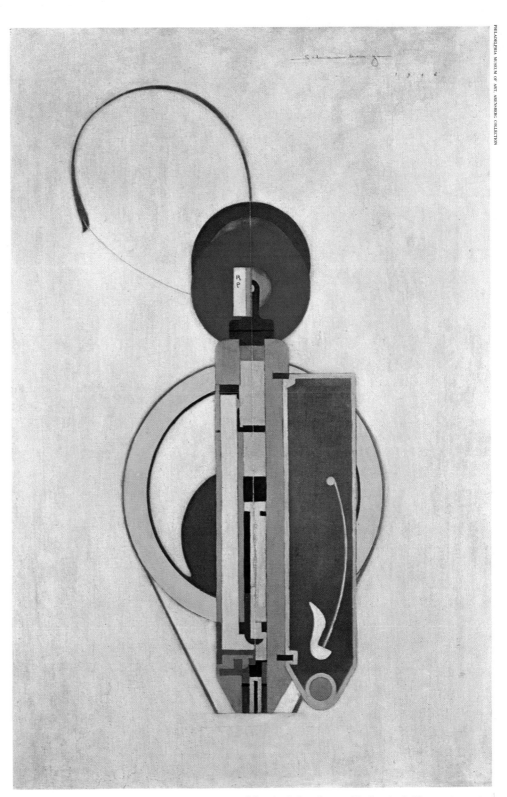

Morton Schamberg: *Mechanical Abstraction*, 1916

was a delusion, the world a poor joke.

Another Dadaist was Morton Schamberg, one of the first American painters to find a suitable subject for art in the appealing geometric precision of machines, as he showed in *Mechanical Abstraction (above)*. Without embellishment or comment, Schamberg depicted machines as objects of intrinsic beauty. He was ambiguous in his attitude toward them, however, fearing them as forces that would dehumanize man. He once caricatured the American idolatry of the functional by mounting plumbing fixtures on a pedestal and calling the "sculpture" *God*.

Arthur B. Carles: *Bouquet Abstraction*, c. 1930

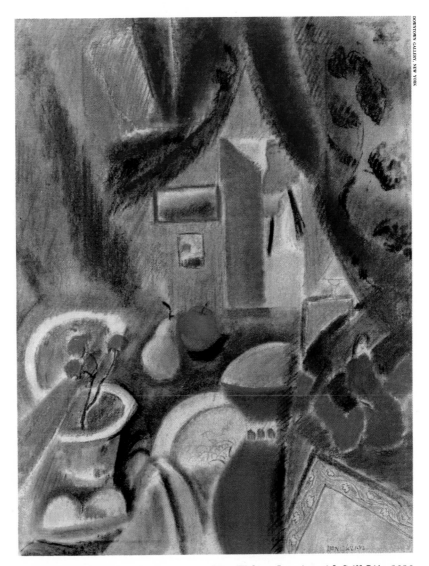

Max Weber: *Interior with Still Life*, 1912

The Fauve manner of using bold, unnaturalistic colors to express subjective feeling profoundly impressed Max Weber and Arthur B. Carles, two Americans who studied painting in Paris with Matisse. Weber was also attracted to other contemporary French styles; in *Interior with Still Life (above)* he integrated a riot of Fauvist colors into a Cubist framework—a triumph of eclecticism. Returning to the United States, Weber carried the message of the new European art with him. He became a close companion of Alfred Stieglitz and was one of the first American moderns to show at his gallery. In 1911 Weber's one-man exhibition there brought forth torrents of critical abuse, giving the abstract painters an uneasy forecast of the reaction awaiting their art at the Armory Show two years later.

A fellow exhibitor at Stieglitz' studio, Carles had become so adept at the Fauve style that his paintings, such as *Bouquet Abstraction (left)*, were often favorably compared to those of Matisse, his teacher. For a number of years before his death in 1952, Carles taught in Philadelphia and continued in his paintings to explore color and form in increasingly masterful abstract works.

Georgia O'Keeffe: *Black Iris*, 1926

54

The sensuous beauty of nature's forms tempted many artists to use them as sources for abstract images. One of the first and finest woman painters in the modern movement, Georgia O'Keeffe created a rich ensemble of soft shapes and muted colors in her extreme close-up view of a black iris shown at the left. Landscape and plant forms constitute a major source of inspiration in her work but always, as in this painting, they serve only as a starting point for a pure and lyrical abstraction that depends neither on sentiment nor intellect.

Arthur Dove was also captivated by nature, creating wholly original work out of the simple shapes of leaves and plants *(below)*. He turned to nature in his life as well as in his art. Abandoning a job as a well-paid magazine illustrator in New York City, he earned a living as a chicken farmer and lobsterman in Connecticut while pursuing his painting. In some of Dove's most haunting works, he attempted to picture such intangibles as the sounds of foghorns; the forms in his landscapes are distilled into pure elements only remotely related to nature. In this respect he made a personal breakthrough, ranking with the work of many of the most advanced European abstractionists.

Arthur Dove: *Plant Forms*, 1915

Charles Demuth: *I Saw the Figure 5 in Gold*, 1928

56

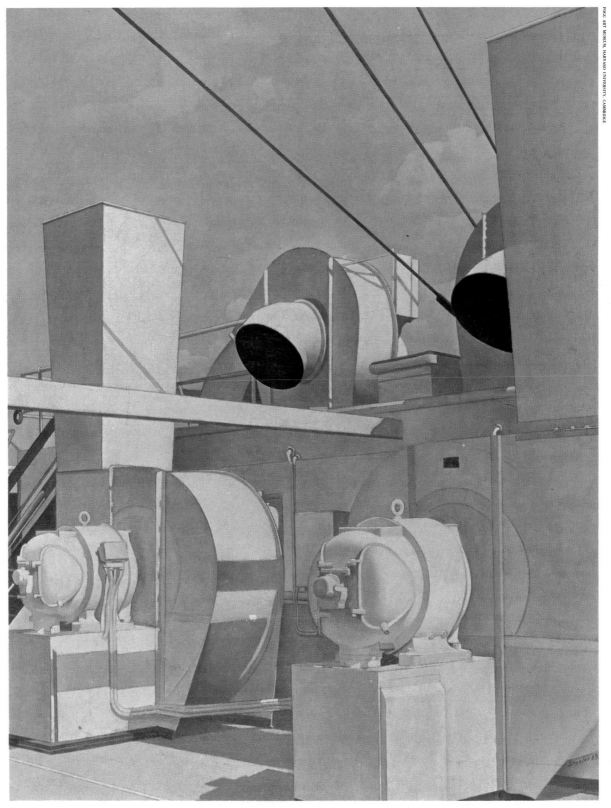

Charles Sheeler: *Upper Deck*, 1929

In his Cubistic painting at left, Charles Demuth took as his title a line from a poem by William Carlos Williams, whose nicknames and initials he also incorporated into the work. Evocative of the rush of a fire truck (Engine Number Five) through city streets, the work delights in the frenetic pace of modern life. Demuth was a member of the Precisionist school, which took mechanistic objects for subject matter. Another Precisionist was Charles Sheeler, whose sharp rendering of the forms on a ship's deck is shown above.

The work of Stuart Davis constitutes a
bridge between the controversial Armory
Show of 1913 and the abstract art of the
1950s. A student at Robert Henri's New York
art school and a budding realist, Davis was
converted to abstractionism at the Armory
Show. He established his credentials with
*Lucky Strike (below)*, a masterpiece of early
abstract style that both echoes Cubist collage
and presages the advertising imagery adopted
by Pop art in the 1960s. Although the tempo
of American life was freshly revealed in
Davis' work, some critics persisted in
belittling his art for its European origins. In
response, Davis painted a dazzlingly original
abstraction in 1956 and wryly entitled it
*Colonial Cubism (opposite)*.

Stuart Davis: *Lucky Strike,* 1921

Stuart Davis: *Colonial Cubism,* 1956

# III

# America Rediscovered

In the 1920s, abstract art won the undivided allegiance of the American art establishment. Most serious artists, trend-conscious collectors and curators of museums saw in abstraction the inventive forms that best captured the rowdy nature of the Jazz Age. In these circles, realism was scorned; it seemed a style hopelessly old-fashioned, inadequate in light of the complexity of American life.

But to a small and voluble group of painters, realism was far from dead. These men believed, on the contrary, that it was the answer to America's search for a true native style. To them, the national art should show Americans in their familiar settings, preferably simple folk realistically portrayed against rural backdrops. Because of this preference in their work, they eventually became known as painters of the American Scene.

Although the American Scene members turned their full attention to the United States and painted its land and people in highly conventional terms, they worked in several different styles. These ranged from the florid elegance of Thomas Hart Benton, who rendered scenes of his beloved Midwest in full-blown curves and lush colors, to the spare, moody, starkly lighted studies of abandoned houses and all-night diners executed by Edward Hopper. John Steuart Curry brought a robust style to views of the customs, people and weather of his native Kansas, while Grant Wood portrayed the people and places of the Midwest at large with wry humor and insight. Younger than the others, Andrew Wyeth continued the realist tradition with crisp, hauntingly evocative paintings that go deeper than the surface of reality to suggest the loneliness of man—in an empty room into which wind-blown curtains fly, in the gable of a Cape Cod house, in a woman asleep on the grass. Wyeth was only a teenager when his colleagues were at the peak of fame and creativity in the 1930s. But like theirs, his work became extremely popular with the general public, his canvases often uniting critic and layman alike in admiration.

American Scene painting was in great part a reaction against abstract art. Some of its exponents, like Grant Wood, avoided public dis-

Ralph Cline, the elderly man posing in his old World War I uniform at left, operates a sawmill near Andrew Wyeth's summer home in Maine. Wyeth persuaded Cline to have his portrait done after agreeing to hold the sittings in an upstairs room at the mill, away from the prying eyes of neighbors. The result is a moving character study of a resilient Yankee, dressed in the proud medals of his youth but with the experiences of a lifetime etched on his face.

Andrew Wyeth: *The Patriot*, 1964

cussion of the fact, but others, notably Benton, lashed out at abstractionism and those who promoted it with a vindictiveness that often degenerated into irrationality. Benton was an early leader of the American Scene painters. A tough, combative man with firm opinions on everything, he was an eloquent speaker and writer, his phraseology often as vivid as his paintings.

Benton never did anything halfway. As a young artist, he was a believer in modern art, traveling to Paris to study at modernism's home and birthplace. Later he was to refer to his stay there in the direct, folksy manner that he had learned in his Missouri country boyhood. Paris to him was "a girl friend to take care of you and run you . . . a lot of talk and an escape into the world of pretense and theory. I wallowed in every cockeyed ism that came along, and it took me 10 years to get all that modernist dirt out of my system. I was merely a roughneck with a talent for fighting, perhaps, but not for painting."

Benton did not reject abstract art immediately on his return to the United States in 1912. He often visited Alfred Stieglitz' studio at 291 Fifth Avenue, where the modernists exhibited their work. But a series of trips around the United States convinced Benton that American artists should seek inspiration in America itself. Americans were engaged in building a new society, continuing to tame the virgin land on which their forefathers had settled. Their lives were crowded with triumphs and heartaches well worth portraying. The abstractionists, Benton felt, were concerning themselves with geometric designs while the reality of America went unpictured.

In his autobiography, Benton stated the problem facing his fellow artists, and proposed a solution. Speaking of Curry, Wood and himself and their rise in popularity in the 1930s he wrote: "We were different in our temperaments and many of our ideas, but we were alike in that we were all in revolt against the unhappy effects which the Armory Show of 1913 had on American painting. We objected to the new Parisian esthetics which was more and more turning art away from the living world of active men and women into an academic world of empty pattern. We wanted an American art which was not empty, and we believed that only by turning the formative processes of art back again to meaningful subject matter, in our cases specifically American subject matter, could we expect to get one."

This commitment to an American art based on common national experience could not have been more direct and honest, but it faced immediate disparagement from the art establishment. In the past, groups of representational genre painters had worked in the United States and had been disparagingly dismissed as quaint depicters of local trivia. Inevitably, the American Scene painters were pigeonholed as "regionalists," as to an extent they were. But they deservedly achieved national attention, in part because of the great convulsion in American history known as the Depression.

As the American Scene painters began to reach the peak of their powers in the early 1930s, factories closed, millions stood in bread lines, and once-confident businessmen were left penniless and shaken.

Working from a live nude model, Thomas Hart Benton completes his version of the Greek myth of Persephone *(page 72)* at the Kansas City Art Institute, where he taught. In the background, some of his students work on their own paintings of the model. Benton's unflinching portrayals of nude women had much to do with the early popularity of his work. The nudity in *Persephone* and *Susanna and the Elders (page 73)* stimulated much righteous indignation—and interest—in the Midwest. The director of the City Art Museum in St. Louis threatened to remove *Susanna* from an exhibition, but reneged. Crowds of people swarmed to the museum to see the painting.

Another group of artists, the Social Realists, also rejected abstractionism and took to direct attacks on social evils *(Chapter Four)*. But the American Scene painters stuck to their paintings of folk legends and uncomplicated views of rural and small-town life, and in them many Americans found a measure of comfort in a time of profound national doubt. These artists offered a stunned public a return to traditional values. In ambitious canvases and sweeping murals, they reasserted America's faith in itself by holding a mirror up to the land. The images in this mirror were often embarrassingly romanticized. In a mural by Curry *(pages 74-75)* the pioneers striding forward to settle the Western plains are so stalwart as to be caricatures. But the mural, like other American Scene works, won wide popularity; Americans needed to be reminded of their conquests in a period when their defeats faced them every day.

The success of the American Scene painters was not, of course, wholly a product of the Depression. To a large segment of the art-loving public, their naturalistic paintings were an overdue, and welcome, relief from modern art. In the past, Americans had been chided for failing to embrace the abstract designs of the modern masters. Bewildered, irritated, bored or simply ignorant of what artists were up to, the public at large neither understood nor was particularly interested in the intentions or merits of modern art. The American Scene artists, however, gave them paintings of people and places they could readily identify —and identify with.

Benton, with his quick grasp of public mood and gift for language, stated it clearly: "After 1929," he wrote, "a new and effective liberalism grew over the country and the battles between that liberalism and the entrenched moneyed groups . . . brought out a new and vigorous discussion of the intended nature of our society. This discussion and the political battles over its findings, plus a new flood of historical writing, concentrated the '30s on our American image. It was this country-wide concentration more probably than any of our artistic efforts which raised Wood, Curry and me to prominence in the national scene. We symbolized esthetically what the majority of Americans had in mind—America itself."

Benton's violent dislike of abstract art led him to blame the nation's tastemakers for the decline in popularity of American Scene painting during the 1940s. "The coteries of highbrows, of critics, college art professors and museum boys, the tastes of which had been thoroughly conditioned by the new esthetics of 20th Century Paris, had sustained themselves in various subsidized ivory towers, and kept their grip on the journals of esthetic opinion all during the [1930s]. These coteries, highly verbal but not always notably intelligent or able to see through momentarily fashionable thought patterns, could never accommodate our popularist leanings. They had, as a matter of fact, a vested interest in esthetic obscurity, in highfalutin symbolisms and devious and indistinct meanings. The entertainment of these obscurities, giving an appearance of superior discernment and extraordinary understanding, enabled them to milk the wealthy ladies who went in for art and the college and museum trustees of the country for the means of support.

"The intellectual aspects of art are not art," he went on, "nor does a comprehension of them enable art to be made. It is in fact the over-intellectualization of modern art and its separation from ordinary life intuitions which have permitted it . . . to remain psychologically tied to the 'public be damned' individualism of the last century and thus in spite of its novelties to represent a cultural lag."

Benton's attacks spread beyond abstraction's artistic limitations and into its "foreign" origins. He leveled ill-tempered personal diatribes against his former friend Stieglitz and the Stieglitz group of abstract artists, calling them "an intellectually diseased lot, victims of sickly rationalizations, psychic inversions, and God-awful self-cultivations."

This brand of demagoguery turned many of Benton's well-wishers away from him. Originally, Robert Henri had been an enthusiastic supporter of American Scene painting, which to a considerable measure followed the trail blazed by him and other members of the Ash Can School. But as the charges leveled against the abstractionists became more and more intemperate, Henri felt compelled to disassociate himself from these extreme views.

While the more influential members of the modern-art circle could laugh off Benton's remarks, his rising popularity made many uneasy. American artists who had spent long years mastering the difficult forms of the modern movement were now being dismissed as "foreign" painters. Under the lash of the new realists, the moderate and judicious Arthur Dove, an abstractionist of the first rank, defended his style of painting. "When a man paints the El, a 1740 house or a miner's shack, he is likely to be called by his critics 'American,'" he said. "These things may be in America, but it's what is in the artist that counts. What do we call 'American' outside of painting? Inventiveness, restlessness, speed, change. . . . A painter may put all these qualities in a still life or an abstraction, and be going more native than another who sits quietly copying a skyscraper." Thoughtful, logical phrases, but neither side was persuaded by logic. The argument heatedly raged on throughout the 1930s.

While Benton and his opponents waged their running battles, other artists quietly went about their work. Edward Hopper, a huge, hulking man, was a taciturn creature of habit who spent his winters painting in a studio on Manhattan's Washington Square and his summers working on the sunny coast of Cape Cod. A former student of Henri, Hopper was so uncompromisingly realistic in his paintings that they became almost surrealist *(pages 84-87)*. He was also realistic in his assessment of the artistic squabbles going on around him. "The question of the value of nationality in art is perhaps unsolvable," Hopper once wrote. "In general it can be said that a nation's art is greatest when it most reflects the character of its people. French art seems to prove this." Acknowledging that American art owed a considerable debt to the artists of France, he rejected the notion that Americans should continue to pursue the French path: "If an apprenticeship to a master has been necessary, I think we have served it. Any further relation of such a character can only mean humiliation to us. After all we are not French and never can be, and any attempt to be so is to deny our inheritance and to try to impose upon ourselves a character that can be nothing but a veneer upon the surface."

Grant Wood, for his part, saw in a regional approach the salvation and renaissance of American art. A quiet man, Wood had studied in Paris before returning to his native Iowa, where he lived the rest of his life. Like most of the American Scene painters, Wood found contentment and inspiration close to home, and he reveled in small-town life. To encourage artists of talent, he advocated competitions among the best painters in each region of the nation, believing that out of such contests would come a national art. Outlining his concept in a letter to the art editor of TIME in 1934, Wood declared: "The great cathedrals of France—in fact, the whole idea back of Gothic architecture—grew out of the competition of cities and towns in the building of churches. . . . As a juror at various state shows in the Middle West, I have found a surprising amount of new talent, needing only the spur of competition to carry it on to a wider field."

Wood himself had burst into prominence from the obscurity of regional painting in 1930 when his now-famous *American Gothic* won a

During the Depression years the American need to bolster its sense of national pride was met to some small degree in the making of a huge monument at Mount Rushmore, South Dakota. Combining the faces of four famous Presidents, the relief was carved from the 1,300-foot-high mountain wall. The monument was the idea of Gutzon Borglum, a sculptor famous for his statues and portrait busts of patriots. Aided by a large work crew, and using jackhammers and dynamite, Borglum completed the first face, Washington's, in 1930. Jefferson was finished in 1936, Lincoln in 1937 and Theodore Roosevelt in 1939 (it was still being worked on when this picture was taken early in the same year). The entire monument cost the taxpayers more than a million and a half dollars—a fortune during the Depression. When questioned about the price, Borglum snapped, "Call up Cheops and ask him how much his pyramid in Egypt cost and what he paid the creator. It was inferior work to Mount Rushmore."

bronze medal at an exhibit mounted by the Art Institute of Chicago. As was often the case with Wood's paintings, *American Gothic* aroused a storm of controversy. Many viewers, particularly his neighbors in Iowa, considered the painting an insulting caricature of simple rural folk. But in time, most of the critics were won over. The writer Christopher Morley expressed what many people felt about the painting. "In those sad and fanatical faces," he wrote, "may be read much, both of what is right and what is wrong with America." Wood, as pithy as always, said of the work and his sitters, his sister and his dentist, "I tried to characterize them honestly, to make them more like themselves than they are in actual life. . . . To me they are basically good and solid people." The public, by and large, accepted Wood's interpretation; although they both come in for some fond caricaturing, *American Gothic* still ranks with Whistler's *Mother* as one of the most popular paintings in America.

Success had not come early or easily to Wood. He was 38 when *American Gothic* won its prize and gained him national attention. For many years he had struggled to master his own style. Even while he lived the artist's life in Paris, sporting a Basque beret and a red beard, a true measure of personal expression had eluded him. He returned to Iowa believing that his greatest artistic inspiration came when "he was milking a cow." But Europe was to provide him with his inspiration after all. In 1928 he was sent to Germany to learn the art of making stained-glass windows in order to fulfill a commission for the Cedar Rapids Veterans Memorial Building. At museums in Munich, Wood was entranced by examples of Flemish primitive art, finding in their rich patterns, fine details and lustrous finishes guides to the style he had been searching for.

*American Gothic,* done after this second trip to Europe, reflects the

In this snapshot the models for Grant Wood's famous *American Gothic* stand beside the original painting. The woman is Wood's sister, Nan; the man is a Cedar Rapids dentist, Dr. B. H. McKeeby, who was a friend of the artist. Wood called the figures in the painting "tintypes from my own family album." The work was inspired not so much by the people as by a house—a low white farmhouse with a peaked gable and a single Gothic window—that Wood saw in southern Iowa. As he later explained, "I imagined American Gothic people with their faces stretched out long to go with this American Gothic house."

Flemish influence, with its scrupulous concern for detail in everything from the precisely drawn Gothic window in the farmhouse behind the couple to the brooch at the woman's throat. The painting secured Wood's position in American art, but the artist continued his fight to win friends for other regional artists.

In this attempt to encourage regional artists to seek national recognition, Wood was joined by the other American Scene painters. But they never realized their goal. In fact, their pleas—and their art—came to command less and less attention. As the Depression eased in the late 1930s the men who portrayed homey American activities began to be generally regarded as sentimental rustics, well intentioned, but very much behind the times. With the advent of World War II the American political isolation and introspection of the '30s was displaced by a renewal of national spirit spurred by the call to arms. Europe was now very much in the forefront of the American consciousness; art that glorified the homestead increasingly came to seem more passé than ever.

Much of the pejorative reaction to abstractionism by the American Scene realists was unjustified. The rejection that came to them, in turn, was equally unfair. These men who tried to instill pride in their own country suffered a fate almost worse than public ridicule—public neglect. Grant Wood died at the age of 50 of cancer, his final wish reflecting his disillusion. He told Benton that if he got well he was going to change his name, go where nobody knew him, and start all over again with a new style of painting. Benton reported that Curry felt a similar sense of despair just before he died in 1946. Benton said to him, "John, you must feel pretty good now, after all your struggles, to know that you have come to a permanent place in American art." Curry replied, "I don't know about that. Maybe I'd have done better to stay on the farm." Benton himself lived on to see abstract art grow into Abstract Expressionism *(Chapter Six)*, a style even more esoteric than that of the Stieglitz "291" group. In the 1950s he said with dismay: "The art of today is the art of the 1920s, which we repudiated!"

The final irony of Benton's frustrations was that one of the artists in the forefront of the Abstract Expressionist movement in the 1940s and '50s was Jackson Pollock *(Chapter Six)*, one of his prize students. Pollock, like Benton, was a tough-minded Westerner full of passion for life and a great talent for painting. He broke away from Benton's realistic art, but the two remained friends. It was typical of the paradoxes of Benton's life that his favorite student would develop into the most famous American abstract painter of his day.

Andrew Wyeth now carries the banner of the American Scene painters and in him the group has perhaps its finest artist. A realist rooted in the rural past of the nation, Wyeth catches with telling accuracy the small but engrossing details of everyday existence. Art critics have called him a "Magic Realist," a phrase perhaps too mystical for his forthright style. But the essence of the word "magic" lingers in his work. His art blends fantasy and reality with such deftness that it defies easy explanation or categorization. Wyeth himself denies that he is simply a realist. "I'm a pure abstractionist in my thought," he once said. "I'm no more like a realist, such as Eakins or Copley, than I'm like the man in the moon." Abstractionist thinking is a major component in the early drafts of his work. He begins each painting with hasty, emotional sketches. From these he builds, creating the mood, the undercurrent of feeling that ripples through his finished paintings.

"I want more than half the story," Wyeth says. "There are some people who like my work because they see every blade of grass. They're seeing only one side of it. They don't see the tone. If you can combine realism and abstraction, you've got something terrific." Wyeth does regularly achieve something terrific. At his best he is able to freeze the essence of a particular moment in a specific place—the ominous sound of distant thunder, the simple dignity of an aging farmhouse.

Wyeth is no stranger to the life unseen. He spent his youth realizing dreams. His father, Newell Converse Wyeth, was a prominent illustrator who achieved considerable success with his drawings for children's classics like *Robin Hood* and *Treasure Island*. He raised his own five children on a large estate in Chadds Ford, Pennsylvania, encouraging their imaginations with games, and their artistic proclivities with lessons. Andrew was the youngest of the children and since school made him "nervous" he was educated at home by tutors. The boy indulged his fantasies playing Robin Hood with his friends, living the lives of the characters his father drew. His early talent for art was bolstered by his father's instructions, but Andrew was not the only talented Wyeth. Three of his brothers and sisters became artists in their own right. His oldest sister, Henriette, later married the American portraitist and painter of New Mexico, Peter Hurd, adding still another distinguished artistic name to the family circle. Andrew's son James, like his father, was a prodigy who is now a recognized artist with several major shows to his credit.

Andrew Wyeth has followed his own father's way of life, wintering in Chadds Ford and summering in Maine. Keeping to his private world, he has never traveled extensively, studied in Europe, or publicly contended with rival artists or schools of art. He has remained content to chart his own small sectors of America. Yet his vivid private visions have not limited his sense of the huge and sprawling land that lies beyond. He is well aware of the American feeling for space and activity. He attains an aura of vastness by first painting his backgrounds, often sweeping views of empty countryside, then almost as an afterthought adding people, generally solitary figures. If he chooses not to show people, he interjects some sign of life—the tracks of a bird in soft ground, or a row of seashells neatly left by some long-ago inhabitant of a now-empty room. The result conveys a special feeling of space and time, an encapsulated history of a place, and a suggestion of its future. If ever an American artist endowed the commonplace with the breadth of universal experience, it is Wyeth. As he depicts seemingly minor events in the life of his subjects, he reveals with immense skill and deep perception the longings and limitations of America and Americans. This was the goal of the American Scene painters.

Thomas Hart Benton: New School Murals (detail), *Oil*, 1930

# Grassroots Artists

As the Depression overtook the United States in the 1930s, one group of artists turned nostalgically inward to picture the traditional verities that they believed had made the nation great and that it had lost. The advent of these American Scene painters was dramatically announced by a powerful set of murals by Thomas Hart Benton *(above and overleaf)*. Completed in 1930 for the New School for Social Research in Manhattan, the murals are crammed with muscular, energetic views of American life.

Thomas Hart Benton: New School Murals (detail), *Mining*, 1930

Thomas Hart Benton: New School Murals (detail), *The Old South*, 1930

Thomas Hart Benton: New School Murals (detail), *Steel*, 1930

Thomas Hart Benton: New School Murals (detail), *City Scenes*, 1930

Thomas Hart Benton: *Persephone*, 1939

**B**enton was a traditionalist who often set classical and Biblical tales in his native rural America. In his version of the Greek legend of Persephone, the goddess of fertility who was abducted by Hades, lord of the underworld, Hades is shown as an aging Missouri farmer *(above)*. The Biblical story of *Susanna and the Elders (opposite)* casts the elders, peeping at Susanna in her bath, as a pair of Ozark rednecks, while the hair style and tweezed eyebrows of Susanna are pure 1930s American. Benton employed traditional techniques as well as subject matter. He preferred the Italian Renaissance method of using egg-yolk tempera as a base for his paints instead of oil. His rounded figures recall the style of Baroque art.

Thomas Hart Benton: *Susanna and the Elders,* 1938

John Steuart Curry: *Justice Defeating Mob Violence*, 1937

John Steuart Curry, like Benton, staged the drama of American life in huge, stirring murals. Two of these works, *Westward Migration (below)* and *Justice Defeating Mob Violence (left)*, were done as decorations for the Department of Justice building in Washington, D.C. Both are highly romanticized works, yet Curry's mastery of theme and his intense involvement in the tumult of a growing nation give them a raw and surging power.

In *Westward Migration* he shows the pioneers pushing forward to tame the wilds from a land already green with crops. The lawlessness that awaits them is suggested by the gun-fighting cowboys; a prairie fire signals that nature too will be a threat. As an old scout in beard and buckskin points the way, the homesteaders are led by a sturdy pioneer father flanked by his wife and baby and his young son.

To honor the Justice Department of the '30s, the mural at left could hardly have been more apt. It shows an exhausted fugitive falling at the feet of a federal judge while a masked lyncher, backed by an irate posse, presses forward with a noose. The judge stays the mob with a raised hand as Army troops stand stolidly in the doorway, symbolizing the widening powers of the U.S. government in assuring justice across the land.

John Steuart Curry: *Westward Migration*, 1936

Curry's view of the world could be heroic, but it was sometimes brutally realistic too. In *Hogs Killing a Rattlesnake* he recalls an incident he witnessed as a boy in Kansas. To recapture the sense of terror he felt then, he adopted a boy's perspective for the picture. Viewed from below, the hogs rear like wild elephants in their strength and fury. Set against massive trees and a lowering sky, the scene seems summoned from some primordial age.

Curry often alternated between such harsh scenes of the rugged life on the plains and the glorification of American sagas. But he never fooled himself about the real purpose of serious art. Like most of the American Scene painters, he was an eloquent man. "Your greatness will not be found in Europe or in New York," he once said, advising students, "or in the Middle West, or in Wisconsin, but within yourself; and realize now that for the sincere artist there is no bandwagon that goes the whole way, no borrowed coat of perfect fit, and no comforter on whose breast to lay your curly head."

John Steuart Curry: *Hogs Killing a Rattlesnake*, 1930

77

Grant Wood brought to American painting a sly wit that prompted both smiles and anger. In *Parson Weems' Fable* he took on the venerable tale of young George Washington chopping down the cherry tree, then honestly owning up to his father. By calling the incident a fable, the artist made clear his opinion of its truth. Moreover, he impishly painted Washington with the body of a six-year-old boy but gave him a head from one of the renowned Gilbert Stuart portraits of the first President. The author of the story, Parson Mason Locke Weems, stands by, pointing toward the scene and gazing at the viewer with a trace of a smile on his lips. For the fun of it, Wood set the action in front of his own red-brick house in Iowa City, Iowa.

Wood had good reason to believe that the cherry-tree story was a fable. Parson Weems, a contemporary of Washington, was famous for his roadside sermons and self-promotion. His *Life of Washington*, published directly after the President's death, was so popular that it ran through more than 70 editions. The original made no mention of the cherry-tree episode; it was added in 1806 in the fifth edition, and Weems claimed that it had been told him "20 years ago by an aged lady who was a distant relative" of Washington. The story had struck such a responsive chord in the national consciousness, however, that Wood's irreverent painting brought down the wrath of a number of self-proclaimed patriots. The artist remained calm, saying only: "I have taken a tip from the good Parson and have used my imagination freely."

Grant Wood: *Parson Weems' Fable*, 1939

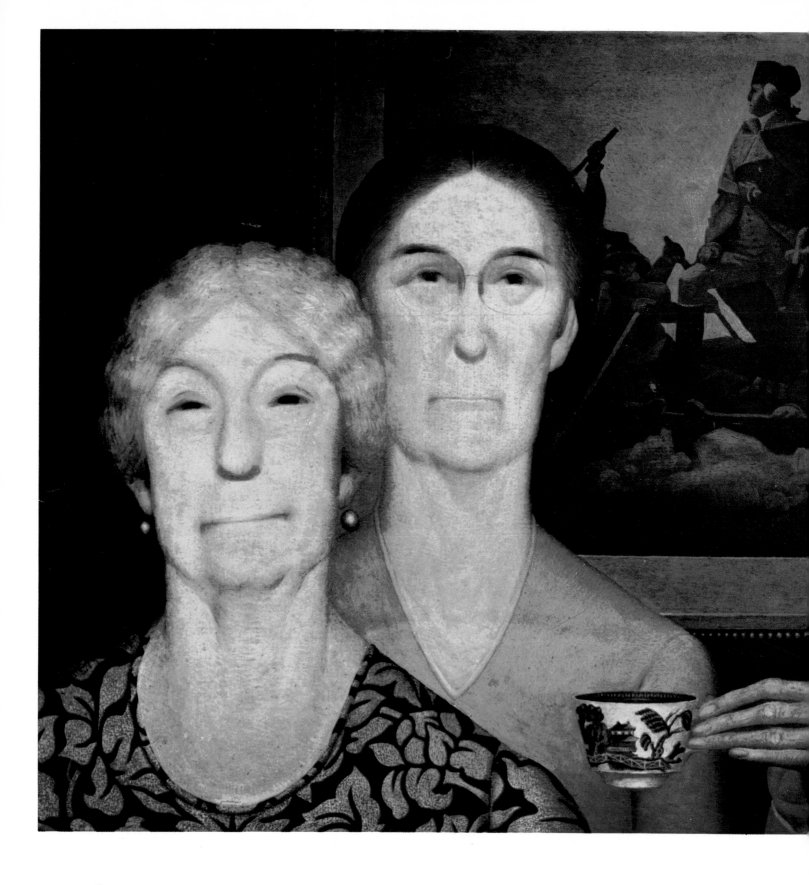

Ignoring the gentle ironies of his *Parson Weems'*
*Fable*, Wood once called *Daughters of Revolution*
*(above)* "the only satire I have ever painted." The
subject of the satire is clear enough; by placing in the
background Emanuel Leutze's familiar painting of
*Washington Crossing the Delaware* Wood left no
doubt he had that patriotic band, the Daughters of

the *American* Revolution, in mind.

Wood had had a teapot-sized feud with the ladies
of the DAR. It began in 1928 after the American
Legion had commissioned him to do a stained-glass
window for the new Cedar Rapids Veterans Memorial,
and had sent him to Europe to learn the technique.
After the window had been installed, some members

Grant Wood: *Daughters of Revolution*, 1932

of the Legion and the DAR belatedly realized that its glass panels had been made in, of all places, Germany —America's enemy only 10 years earlier. Indignantly, they refused to allow the window to be dedicated. Wood quietly took his revenge with *Daughters*. As is often the case, those outraged by something describe it with more truth than the creator ever would.

Members of the Sons of the American Revolution said the painting showed "three sour-visaged, squint-eyed and repulsive-looking females, represented as disgustingly smug and smirking because of their ancestral heroes of the American Revolution." Wood's own comment was deadpan. He called the work "a pretty rotten painting. Carried by its subject matter."

JOHN KANE

In colonial days, artists often painted both houses and canvases. John Kane continued this tradition. He turned to painting—houses and works of art—late in life after a train accident severed his left leg below the knee and kept him from his job as a street paver. He loved to go on weekends to the outskirts of Pittsburgh, where he lived, and paint landscapes like the one at left. Kane brought to his new hobby a childlike awareness, revealing the familiar with wide-eyed pleasure. "We can learn something from nature each time we go out," he said. "Each time we hear the robin say, 'Paint me, John. Paint me.'"

Kane was 67 before he received his first official recognition when one of his paintings was shown at an exhibition in Pittsburgh. Even after he gained wide public attention, he remained a Sunday painter. One of his few problems was the kibitzing of curious boys. "I have always loved boys," he said. "But I cannot abide their jeers and comical suggestions. They think they are being funny at the expense of a poor old man like myself who tries to concentrate on the beauty that takes his very soul." Yet for all his troubles with boys, Kane still painted them with affection (below).

John Kane: *Turtle Creek Valley, No. 1*, c. 1930

John Kane: *4th of July Parade*, c. 1928

Edward Hopper: *Seven A.M.*, 1948

The laconic, brooding Edward Hopper was engrossed by commonplace scenes other artists chose to ignore. His vision of America was a store before opening hours *(above)*, an awkward old house standing in solitary dignity *(right, top)*, an isolated gas station with one elderly attendant puttering around *(right, bottom)*. His style, refined and reduced to the edge of bleakness and severity, relentlessly focused on a single theme, makes a Hopper painting glow in the mind like a suddenly remembered moment.

Paradoxically, Hopper developed his highly personal style by avoiding painting for many years.

He studied art in Paris in 1906, but kept to himself, seldom entering art circles. Returning to America, he sold a canvas at the 1913 Armory Show, but then virtually abandoned painting for 10 years and devoted his time to commercial illustration. When he took up painting full time again at 43, he approached it as a mature man with a definite viewpoint. Having worked with etchings, a form particularly suited to his emphasis on light and shadow, he turned to watercolors and then to oils. The oils gave him added range, but it was his original view of the world that elevated his work.

Edward Hopper: *House by the Railroad*, 1925

Edward Hopper: *Gas*, 1940

Hopper was preoccupied with loneliness. He found it everywhere, even in the palatial movie houses of the 1930s, where people sought refuge from the dreary grind of the Depression years in the fantasies of the screen. In *New York Movie (right)*, each individual —the customers sitting in their seats, the bored, smartly uniformed usherette—appears lost in his own private thoughts, unaware of one another or even the motion-picture screen. A stillness, a vague emptiness, seems to hang over the work.

Searching for subject matter, Hopper spent much of his life traveling about the country, letting impressions gather in his memory. Periodically he would return to New York City or Cape Cod, where he maintained studios, to paint. His affection for man-made objects, usually pictured with a few or no people nearby, led him to paint quiet lighthouses, empty bridges and fragmented city views in which the buildings took on more importance than the occupants. This infatuation with the constructions of man sometimes led him into odd predicaments. When visiting New Mexico, Hopper was disoriented by the breathtaking beauty of the countryside. He wandered bemused through the majestic settings, searching for a scene to paint. At last he discovered something worth a watercolor: an abandoned locomotive.

Edward Hopper: *New York Movie*, 1939

The man of the soil is pictured in precise and
knowing detail, his round face weathered,
his clothes old but still functional. He stands in front
of a shed he has built with old boards gathered while
cleaning up other people's property. His name is

Adam Johnson and he is a neighbor of Andrew Wyeth
in the little town of Chadds Ford, Pennsylvania.

In the winter Wyeth paints the people and places
around Chadds Ford; in the summer he does the same
in Cushing, Maine. As he puts it, "I want to show

Andrew Wyeth: *Adam*, 1963

Americans what America is like." In so doing, Wyeth infuses his work with a haunting sense of what America is, and was, a mood that often sends a shiver of recognition through the viewer. In the sunlit side of a house on the Maine coast *(overleaf)* he evokes a feeling of weather-beaten Yankee strength. In another Maine painting *(page 91)* he suspends a magic moment of summertime, as a hound warily raises its head at the first far-off rumbling of thunder, while Wyeth's wife continues her nap in the grass.

Andrew Wyeth: *Weatherside*, 1965

Andrew Wyeth: *Distant Thunder*, 1961

# IV

# The Social Realists

Black artist Jacob Lawrence
well knew the realities of life
in the ghetto when he painted
this Harlem street scene. Like
many of his contemporaries,
Lawrence grew up in city
slums and his work conveys the
strident vitality as well as the
squalor of overcrowded
tenement living, where the
people spend much of their
time on the stoops and
sidewalks outside their homes.
Here he adds a symbolic
comment by showing a
basement stonecutter's shop,
whose gravemarkers provide a
constant reminder of death.

Jacob Lawrence: *Tombstones*, 1942

When Franklin Delano Roosevelt became President in 1933, he faced
the enormous task of pulling together a country that appeared very
nearly to have destroyed itself. Agriculture was in desperate straits as
markets crumbled and the nation's breadbasket became a dust bowl.
At least a quarter of the labor force was unemployed. The once-busy
cities were grinding to a stop. Revolution, not prosperity, loomed just
around the corner.

In his inaugural address Roosevelt attempted to rally a demoralized
American people with the ringing, unforgettable words: "The only
thing we have to fear is fear itself." And, indeed, by enacting a series
of unprecedented reforms, the New Deal gradually put the economy
on the way to recovery. But while corporations—which had suffered a
two-billion-dollar loss in 1932—showed a profit of five billion dollars
by 1936, labor lagged sadly behind: eight million people were still
out of work. A new, insidious force, moreover, rose to menace the
nation from outside: the totalitarian regimes that had come to power
abroad threatened to bring about what Roosevelt called an "epidemic
of world lawlessness."

In reaction to this nightmare world, many American artists rejected
the fashionable, intellectual abstractions that attracted gallerygoers of
the day to paint perfectly real, and recognizable, subjects. But while
painters like Thomas Hart Benton and Grant Wood emphasized the
nostalgic virtues of an idealized rural past *(Chapter III)*, a group
called the Social Realists attacked, head on, the injustices and de-
humanization of industrial and urban life. To a man, they believed that
art and the artist must be engaged with the contemporary world; their
vigorous paintings might have been campaign posters for the active
reform movements that swept through the United States in the 1930s.
The first members of the Social Realist group—led by Ben Shahn,
Moses Soyer and his brothers Raphael and Isaac, Reginald Marsh,
Philip Evergood and Peter Blume—were born around the turn of the
century. Younger men who came of age in the Depression years—
notably Jack Levine, Jacob Lawrence and George Tooker—carried the

Dorothea Lange: *California*, 1939

John Vachon: *Missouri*, 1940

Ben Shahn: *Arkansas*, 1938

tradition through the changing conditions of the following decades.

From 1933 onward, the creativity of these and other artists was reinforced by a variety of government bureaus, including the Farm Security Administration, the Federal Housing Administration and a dozen others. Most important of all were the programs of the Works Progress Administration. Specifically designed to offer financial relief to artists in many fields, WPA projects put them to work at monthly wages, using their talents for the public good. For the first time in American history, the government was spending taxpayers' money to support creative individuals, no matter how talented—and

Carl Mydans: *Tennessee,* 1935

Arthur Rothstein: *Kansas,* 1936

Russell Lee: *Southeast Missouri,* 1938

American governmental support of the arts during the Depression, which took the form of employing artists on a variety of national projects, was broadened to include photographers in 1935. Under the direction of the Farm Security Administration, a group of outstanding photographers, including Dorothea Lange and the painter Ben Shahn, traveled around the country to produce a stunning document of rural poverty, from which the examples at the left are taken. Shahn later returned to his easel, and Vachon, Rothstein and Mydans went on to become highly successful magazine photographers.

some were pretty mediocre—while they practiced their crafts. Architects designed housing projects. Photographers pictured the tragedies of ruined farmers and eroded land. Writers compiled state and regional histories. Composers and playwrights were commissioned to create symphonies and plays, which were then brought to people who had previously known only the secondhand pleasures of recorded music and the movies. Painters, for their part, were similarly commissioned by the government to cover the walls of public buildings with murals and supplied pictures for small-town museums, schools and traveling exhibitions.

Such broad-scale government support confirmed the Social Realists' belief that art is an integral part of society. Their aims were more sharply defined at the first Artists' Congress in 1936. Addressing more than 300 painters, designers, sculptors and photographers gathered in New York, the writer Lewis Mumford declared that fascism, social inequities and economic depression were enemies of human culture. "The time has come," he said, "for the people who love life and culture to form a united front . . . to be ready to protect and guard—if necessary, fight for—the human heritage which we, as artists, embody." The artist's moral responsibility was now greater than a simple duty to his talent, to create solely because he was gifted, as Gauguin once succinctly put it.

The major painters of the Social Realist group came from widely diverse backgrounds: some were the products of exclusive prep schools and Ivy League universities, others grew up amid the corrosive brutality of Jewish and black ghettos in East Coast cities. Their styles, too, were so different that some art historians still classify them not under "Social Realism" but under quite different headings: Expressionist, Magic Realist, Surrealist-influenced. Few of them, in fact, could be described as strictly "realistic" painters. They frequently heightened colors for emotional impact, exaggerated features as a cartoonist does, or distorted physical scale to achieve emphasis. Nevertheless, their subject matter was as harshly real as a battlefield photograph, and the technical devices they used to drive home their points were easily understood by a public that had long been conditioned to posters and advertisements. But no matter how much their individual styles or backgrounds diverged, they all expressed a common passion for social reform. In a way they returned to the Puritanical esthetic attitude of America's early settlers, to whom art without some "higher" moral purpose was anathema.

The personification of this moralistic point of view was Ben Shahn, a zealot in the early wave of Social Realism and a lion in defense of justice. Sometimes more propagandist than painter, Shahn was born in Lithuania and raised in a Brooklyn slum. After attending classes at New York University, the City College of New York and the National Academy of Design, Shahn went to Paris to study in the late 1920s. He was back home on a visit in 1927 when Nicola Sacco and Bartolomeo Vanzetti, two Italian immigrants, were executed in Massachusetts for the murders of a paymaster and a guard in a holdup in a Boston suburb. The prosecution's evidence had been flimsy—one woman witness stuck to her identification of Sacco even when cross-examination brought out that she had been a considerable distance from the scene of the crime and had caught only a fleeting glimpse of the culprits as they sped away in a car. But both men were avowed anarchists—Vanzetti, in particular, was eloquent in defense of his convictions—and in the midst of a nationwide Red scare, a jury found them guilty of the crime. The case aroused worldwide as well as national protest, and in 1931 Shahn began to execute a series of bitter studies on the subject *(pages 102-103)*. Shown in 1932, they were his first success, placing him squarely in the front rank of Social Realism. In later years Shahn himself, however, rejected such pigeonholing. "I prefer to call it personal realism. The distinction is that social realism is dictated from the outside; personal realism comes from your own guts."

Shahn went on to spend several years as a painter and photographer for the Farm Security Administration, depicting both in murals and on film the efforts of the agency to deal with the plight of migratory workers throughout the country. The photographic documentary techniques he learned there, coupled with his studies abroad and a youthful apprenticeship as a lithographer, gave him an extraordinary flexibility. In time he could paint anything in the manner he felt best suited to his message, as he was to demonstrate in later years with such work as *The Welders (page 113)*. Shorn of the intricacies of symbolism he used in the Sacco-Vanzetti series, it is a clear call for racial equality that anyone can understand.

One unexpected result of the mass unemployment of the '30s—a subject that caught the imagination and the brush of Shahn's contemporary, Raphael Soyer—was an empty, even grotesque victory for feminists. Women could often find a job, however miserable, while their husbands and fathers, the traditional breadwinners, could not —and were humiliated by their newly dependent role. Some of these men found it unbearable to eat at a table they could not supply and simply walked out, drifting hopelessly across the country and often congregating in aimless crowds in cities like New York with other men unable to find work. Soyer portrayed such "forgotten men" with gentle understanding in canvases like *Reading from Left to Right (page 101)*, whose bitterly ironic title reflected the standard newspaper means of identifying dignitaries in photographs. He is even better known for his pictures of the city's tired working girls and women, whose physical and mental exhaustion is all too plainly written on their faces. In them is encapsulated Soyer's belief that painting "must describe and express people, their lives and times"—a conviction that virtually sums up Social Realism.

The same philosophy and the same interest in the victims of economic collapse animated the work of Reginald Marsh. "Go out into the street, stare at the people. Go into the subway, stare at the people," Marsh exhorted young artists in search of inspiration. The people he stared at during the '30s were often such desolate debris of the Depression as the city dwellers huddling on *The Park Bench (pages 104-105)*. Paradoxically, this Paris-born child of the Establishment became the supreme chronicler of New York's street life in the period.

His parents, both well-known artists, sent Marsh to Lawrenceville and Yale, where he began his career as an illustrator. After graduation he worked for a few years on the staff of the New York *Daily News*, and in 1925 became one of the original staff members of *The New Yorker* magazine. Later that year he went to Europe to study such classical masters as Rubens and Michelangelo, whose sweeping compositions and full-bodied forms he later emulated.

By the mid-'30s Marsh was known as America's foremost painter of the tawdry gaieties and dreary shabbiness of the city. His reportorial studies of subway straphangers, burlesque houses, dime-a-dance halls and jam-packed summer beaches convey his immense gusto for the anonymous crowd and, simultaneously, a delicate sense of each individual's isolation in it. Marsh was also entirely capable of cruel satire, as he showed when he painted patrons of the opera preening in furs and jewels during the bitter winter of 1936; his smug debutantes and dowagers and their escorts are far less sympathetically portrayed than the blowziest strippers or fattest bathers in his burlesque and Coney Island paintings.

Coney Island fascinated Marsh; he described it as "crowds of people in all directions, without clothing, moving—like the great compositions of Michelangelo and Rubens." In later years, as honors piled upon him, Marsh mourned that Coney was losing its flavor: "The bunions and varicose veins and the flat chests are gone. Now there are only Marilyn Monroes." For a while after his death in 1954, Marsh's reputation faded; his paintings were condemned as too specialized, too topical—and far too dependent on the outmoded technique of the old masters he revered. But his trenchant record of city life was too vivid to remain in limbo. His work caught the spirit of New York so brilliantly that it has escaped the trap of time.

Like Marsh, Philip Evergood broke from a privileged background to find inspiration among the common people. But his meticulously researched paintings of current events—like *American Tragedy*, a study of the massacre of steelworkers in 1937 *(pages 106-107)*—are brutal indictments of social evils, rather than subtly ironic records of his time. Born in New York but educated at Eton and Cambridge—which he left in 1921 at the age of 20 to paint full time—Evergood wandered and studied for 10 years before concentrating on the labor problems of his afflicted homeland.

The time was ripe for such a subject: organized labor, long the underdog, was on its way to unprecedented victories, and the public temper was all for it. Unions were winning increasing recognition and contracts, even with such hard-nosed corporate holdouts as General Motors and United States Steel. *Pins and Needles*, an amateur musical written and performed by members of the International Ladies' Garment Workers' Union, and intended solely as a short-run entertainment for the ILGWU membership, became a smash hit in New York. After rave reviews, it ran for four years, breaking the current record; its wry humor, typified by the heroine's lyric plea, "Sing Me a Song of Social Significance," was so timely that it became part of the national idiom.

In spite of his European education, Evergood was proud of his American heritage, as can be seen in his picture of an unconquerable, bright-eyed old woman sitting amid the wreckage of her New England home after the 1938 hurricane. All the serene old lady has managed to save from the storm is a well-thumbed Bible, but her courage is made clear, not only by her erect composure but by the painting's title: *My Forebears Were Pioneers*. "I value structure, honesty, humor, love for my fellow-man above all else," Evergood once said. "I want my pictures to affect people on the inside."

While the federal government continued through the '30s to enact sweeping social reforms, organized crime reinforced its old partnership with corrupt local politicians. A dozen years of Prohibition had inured the once morally irreproachable middle class to lawbreaking; many a distinguished citizen boasted of being on first-name terms with his bootlegger. Romanticized by movies like *Scarface* and *Little Caesar*, the gangsters whose tentacles had spread across the land in the '20s won a sneaking admiration. People who could imagine no end to their drab chores avidly followed wide newspaper coverage of the headlong careers of criminals like Bonnie and Clyde and John Dillinger. What if they did die at the end? At least they had looted, lived and smashed out at dreary regimentation.

The Social Realists would have none of that philosophy. Marsh early displayed the horror of real-life crime; his *The Death of Dillinger*, commissioned by LIFE in 1940, is not only one of his evocative street scenes but an accurate picture of the moment when FBI agents cornered and killed the criminal. There is nothing romantic in Marsh's depiction of Dillinger's death. As the bullets rip into the killer, Marsh's message sounds clear and cold: the wages of sin is death. Similarly, the hypocritical mourners Jack Levine depicted in *Gangster's Funeral (page 108)* might be actors in a movie scene, but his needle-sharp satire in this and other paintings expresses the anger of an idealistic young man who was exposed to political corruption in South Boston and nearby Roxbury when he was growing up.

As the '30s wore on, the attention of most Americans remained focused inward; the country was desperately intent on redeeming despoiled natural resources like the Great Plains farmlands and giving a measure of dignity and security to labor. The ugly threat of fas-

Jack Levine's satiric pen remained sharp even after the Depression was over, as can be seen in these sketches made at the 1968 Democratic National Convention in Chicago. Working on assignment as an artist for TIME magazine, Levine caught the drowsy look of delegates trying unsuccessfully to listen to endless speeches *(left)*. Outside the convention hall, he sketched the quite different mood of the police, wearing helmets and holding clubs, as they stand ready for trouble before a barbed wire fence *(above)*. The expected assaults on the hall by young dissenters never came, but the Chicago convention ended in a riot as students and police clashed in the streets.

cism seemed remote. Creative artists were among the first to expose the danger of the totalitarian trend abroad. Even before such anti-fascist plays as Robert Sherwood's *Idiot's Delight* reached Broadway to win the Pulitzer Prize of 1936, the Social Realist painter Peter Blume had recognized the burgeoning danger of totalitarianism. In Rome on a fellowship in 1934, Blume began *The Eternal City (pages 110-111)*, an ironic attack on Premier Benito Mussolini and his regime's rape of Rome and Italy.

The warnings of Blume and others, however, went largely unheeded in America, until the threat of fascism finally exploded into war. When the United States became directly involved after Pearl Harbor, many of its painters joined their fellow citizens in the immense job at hand, enlisting in the Army and Navy, putting their skills to work as combat artists, photographers or camouflage experts, or designing posters to encourage military recruitment, the sale of government bonds to help finance the war effort, and the welding of national solidarity. World War II was itself a grim enough training ground for Social Realism. And it was not long before a whole array of postwar problems materialized to command attention: the Cold War; a new, hot war in Korea; the repressive atmosphere of the McCarthy era, which responded hysterically to the threat of world Communism; the ever-present specter of nuclear holocaust.

In the postwar era, artists, like other Americans, attempted once again to respond to society's ills, particularly to newly recognized injustices of race and the continuing decline of the quality of life in cities. George Tooker, for one, chillingly showed the prisonlike character of urban existence in the faces of human beings daily engulfed in the anonymous subway *(pages 114-115)*. His view of New York, by contrast with Marsh's rejoicing in the city's people, however much they might be bent by the continuing degradation of the Depression years, was essentially brutal. He painted the lonely frustration of the period, not only in such works as *The Subway*, but in such equally depressing renderings of reality as *Government Bureau*. There, human beings hopelessly tangle with faceless members of officialdom who are obviously never going to find the right rubber stamp, nor even the number of the office next door where the stamp is to be found. Jacob Lawrence, a distinguished black artist, chronicled the life of the ghetto and the struggle of his people for equal rights *(page 92)*. His preoccupation with Negro problems was shared by other, younger painters who poignantly, often angrily, depicted the predicament of black Americans in a white society.

Whatever their subjects, or however they held them up to view, these latter-day Social Realists carried on the faith of their predecessors: a deep, sometimes naïve, sometimes bitter, but always passionate belief that art must show the truth, and that when it does, society will react. In this respect they are activists in a thoroughly American tradition. Their best works not only serve to call attention to the particular despairs and evils of their times, but stand, too, as lasting statements about the human condition.

Raphael Soyer: *Reading from Left to Right*, 1936

# Paintings of Protest

The work of the Social Realists ranged from the problems of the unemployed in the Depression years to the pressures of urban life in the 1960s. In this 1936 painting by Raphael Soyer, defeated men huddle in ill-fitting, shabby overcoats on a street corner, their homelessness attested by the bedroll carried by the man at right. Soyer once declared that he felt "embarrassed when people tell me my works show sympathy for people." Soyer's characterization, nevertheless, betrays his heartfelt compassion for the misery of people overwhelmed by economic circumstances they cannot hope to influence.

101

I got to thinking about the Sacco-Vanzetti case. . . .
Ever since I could remember I'd wished that I'd been
lucky enough to be alive at a great time—when
something big was going on. . . . And suddenly I
realized I was. . . . Here was something to paint!" In
these words Ben Shahn recalled the moment when he
found his role as a painter of social protest. Five years
after the death of Nicola Sacco and Bartolomeo

Vanzetti, the two Italian immigrants who were
electrocuted in 1927 for the alleged murders of a
paymaster and a payroll guard, Shahn completed a
series of 23 studies on the subject. He returned to it
many times, executing a large mural based on the case
as late as 1967. In his 1932 painting above, a group of
working-class demonstrators *(left)* demands freedom
for the prisoners. Next to them the tiny figure of the

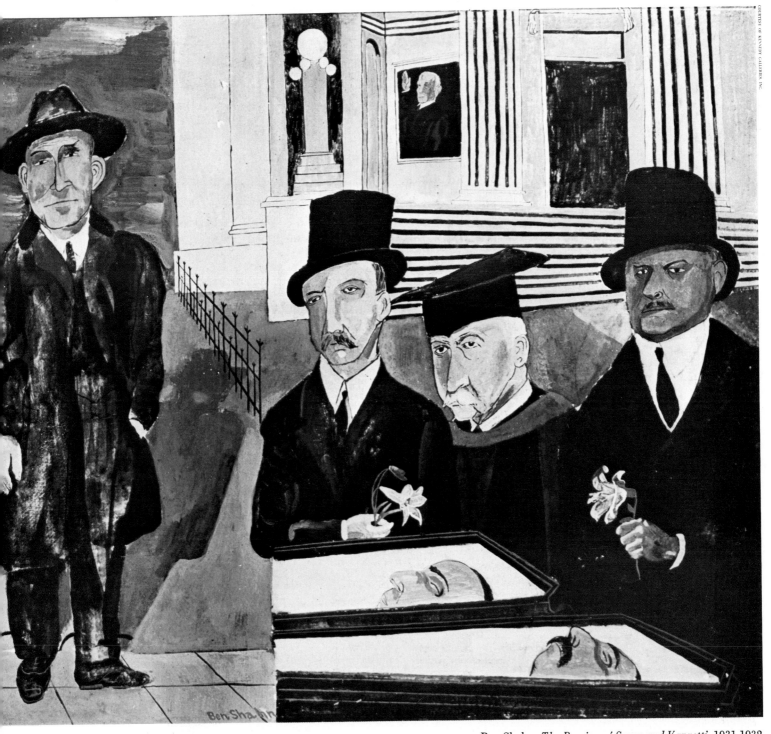

Ben Shahn: *The Passion of Sacco and Vanzetti*, 1931-1932

Massachusetts governor, Alvan Fuller, refuses to stay the execution. He is dwarfed by the towering figures of the defendants, Vanzetti, in the cap, and Sacco.

At far right, standing impassively over the dead men's coffins, is the committee of prominent men—a judge and the presidents of Harvard and the Massachusetts Institute of Technology—who investigated the trial, found it fair and upheld the death sentence. They made this decision despite widespread feeling across the country that Sacco and Vanzetti were simply the victims of the national Red scare and a wave of anti-immigrationism. In the background hangs a portrait of the trial judge, Webster Thayer, who during the six years between the verdict and the execution consistently denied all motions for a new trial.

Reginald Marsh: *The Park Bench*, 1933

Lassitude, born of too little to eat, nothing to do and no place to go, afflicts the occupants of *The Park Bench* by Reginald Marsh. Like his friend Raphael Soyer, Marsh often painted New York City's indigent, but with a different emphasis. Where the weary faces in Soyer's *Left to Right (page 101)* convey a sense of each man's discouragement, Marsh has blurred the features of his bench sitters, muting their individuality.

Famous for his studies of Coney Island revelers, Marsh excelled in capturing the spirit of the crowd. In this painting he turned his talents to a somber theme; the torpor of the jobless was a widespread phenomenon of the Depression years. Newspapers headlining world events figure in many Marsh paintings and underline his absorption in the life of his times. In this canvas a man reads the Communist *Daily Worker*, which reached its circulation peak of 100,000 in the 1930s.

Philip Evergood: *American Tragedy*, 1937

**P**hilip Evergood's *American Tragedy* bitterly commemorates a terrible moment in American labor history. On Memorial Day, 1937, in South Chicago, more than a thousand Republic Steel workers and their families went to a meeting of the steelworkers' union, which was fighting for recognition. Someone called for a protest march to the plant's gates and the workers set off under the warm sun, jaunty in their spring holiday clothes. Two blocks from their destination, they were met by an advancing blue phalanx of 200 city police. Suddenly the police threw tear-gas bombs into the crowd. As the mist spread they rushed on the marchers, charging, as an eyewitness recalled, "like a bunch of demons," swinging billy clubs and firing their guns. The marchers fled across an open field, with the police in pursuit.

Evergood used newspaper photographs and accounts in planning his picture. The meticulousness of his research is evident in the painting: of the 10 marchers who were killed, nine were white and one *(lower left)* was black; of the nearly 100 persons injured, one woman *(left)* was shot in the back. But the picture derives its power from the depth of the artist's indignation. The central figures of the man protecting his pregnant wife (armed with a tree branch, as some of the marchers were) from the onslaught of the coarse-featured, savage police express Evergood's outrage and his sympathy with the workers. The Memorial Day Massacre dealt a heavy blow to the growing labor movement at Republic Steel; not until 1942 did the steelworkers win a contract from the company.

In Jack Levine's *The Feast of Pure Reason (right)*, a crooked cop and a venal politician confer with a cutaway-clad banker. The painting's sardonic title makes its meaning clear. The phrase was first used by the 18th Century satirist Alexander Pope to describe an imaginary chat between himself and the few statesmen of his time whom he respected; James Joyce later used it in his monumental novel *Ulysses* to describe the citizens of Dublin running amuck in a riot incited by their heads of state and church. Levine, like Joyce, is sounding a warning to the people to beware betrayal by unscrupulous men of power. Fifteen years after he painted it, Levine said that *The Feast* was the "work which is most like me." But more recently, discussing his tendency as time went on to see life in shades of gray rather than black and white, he called it a picture that "was fired out of one barrel" and was based "on the bitter assumptions of a boy of 22." Levine's mellowing is evident in *Gangster's Funeral (below)*. Completed in 1953, it conveys an almost comic tone, rather than a harshly bitter indictment of the gangland mourners.

Jack Levine: *Gangster's Funeral*, 1952-1953

Jack Levine: *The Feast of Pure Reason*, 1937

In 1932, Italy's Fascist dictator, Benito Mussolini, observed his 10th anniversary as chief of state. His likeness, often captioned "Mussolini is always right," was on display everywhere. One day as Peter Blume, a 26-year-old artist who was in Italy on a Guggenheim grant, stood watching the light play on the ancient Forum in Rome, he decided to paint a picture based on what he believed Mussolini's Fascism had meant to Italy. The result, completed in 1937 after Blume's return to the United States, was *The Eternal City (right)*.

The painting is a surrealist cityscape, dominated by a papier-mâché, jack-in-the-box Mussolini. The dictator pops out of the floor of the Colosseum above the heads of two of his supporters, an unsavory capitalist and a thug wearing the black shirt of Mussolini's Fascist party. On the far left two oblivious tourists gape at an image of Christ that has been bedecked with jewelry and set in a grotto strewn with ornate offerings. A citizen of modern Rome—a crippled female beggar—sits beside fragments of the city's classical past, a shattered statue of lovers *(foreground)*. In the central background, crowds stream into the Roman Forum, where soldiers are starting to mutiny against their officers—a hopeful call for revolution against the regime.

In 1939, a leading Washington, D.C., museum, fearful of reactions to the picture's political content, refused to exhibit it. Artists' groups protested the action, but Blume had to settle for displaying his painting in a small art gallery. In the spring of 1943, a few months before U.S. troops invaded the Italian mainland and two years before Mussolini's death at the hands of his own people, *The Eternal City* was bought by the New York Museum of Modern Art.

Peter Blume: *The Eternal City*, 1934-1937

Ben Shahn's involvement in social problems continued throughout his career. He was among the U.S. artists who produced posters for government and private agencies during World War II. In 1943 and 1944 he did five posters for the CIO's Political Action Committee, one of which, *The Welders (below)*, became familiar to millions of people. The lithograph's slogan read, "For full employment after the war

—register, vote!" It was distributed during the PAC's highly successful 1944 registration drive among union members, aimed at electing a prolabor Congress and the re-election of Franklin Roosevelt. The poster reflected a breakthrough in civil rights: the wartime shortage of manpower forced many industries to drop their color barriers; black and white worked side by side under Presidential orders banning discrimination.

Ben Shahn: *The Welders*, 1944

George Tooker's dreamlike pictures often deal with the plight of the city dweller—his anonymity, isolation and sense of powerlessness in the face of the geometrically increasing pressures of urban life. In *The Subway*, the people glance fearfully around their cagelike environment. The low ceiling presses down on them and the cold fluorescent light bleaches their color to an unnatural pallor. The claustrophobic effect is heightened by the appearance of the revolving exit gate at right: at first glance, its long bars seem to form

a crisscrossing barrier to escape. Tooker frequently employs repetition as a device to enhance the eerie quality of his pictures. Here the two men in hats behind the central figure of the woman are the same man, the three women behind the exit gate are the same woman, and the young man in the raglan overcoat *(right, center)* is echoed three times by the figures in the phone booths at left (this man, a stylized portrait of the artist, appears in other Tooker paintings as well).

George Tooker: *The Subway,* 1950

To my Manguch
Gerry

# V

# A Debt
# to Europe

America began to establish itself as the home of modern art in the
1930s. Formerly, American painters had been required to travel
abroad to find out what was happening on the frontiers of experimental art. But in the '30s and early '40s many foreign artists suddenly arrived in the United States. There were several reasons for this exodus
from Europe: the Depression, which lingered in Europe longer than it
did in the United States; repressive political regimes in countries like
Germany; the threat of war and the coming of war itself.

Some of these European artists came for only a few years; many remained permanently. But no matter the length of their stay, their
presence in the United States was enormously stimulating to American painters, especially the young. For the first time it became possible for large numbers of American artists to see the work of Europeans in depth, talk with the painters and, in some cases, study under
them. American art was greatly enriched by this infusion of new talent.
As a result two new and distinct styles—Geometric Abstraction and
Surrealism—emerged in America.

Among the first painters who came to the United States early in the
'30s were two of the finest and most influential teachers of art in modern times—Hans Hofmann, and Josef Albers. Albers was a master of
Geometric Abstraction, a style that blended the angular shapes of geometry—rectangles, squares, triangles—with colors balanced to gen-
erate a deep sense of harmony. Hofmann, an abstractionist who had
begun teaching in Munich in 1915, spent the summer of 1930 as a
visiting professor at the University of California at Berkeley. He returned the following summer to teach at Berkeley and then settled permanently in the East in 1932, the year before Hitler came to power in
Hofmann's native Germany. Albers, who had been one of the leading
masters at Germany's advanced Bauhaus school, emigrated in 1933
when the Nazis forced the school's closing. He was soon followed by a
distinguished group of Bauhaus teachers and architects, including
Ludwig Miës van der Rohe, Walter Gropius, Marcel Breuer, Laszlo
Moholy-Nagy and Herbert Bayer.

The influence of the Bauhaus masters on American architecture and design is virtually incalculable. Partly based on Miës van der Rohe's provocative dictum, "Less is more," Bauhaus style promulgated an elegant simplicity, functional geometric shapes and the increased use of technology. These influences crept slowly into the architecture and the general visual style of American life. Their effect on the teaching of painting became evident more quickly.

By 1934 Hofmann had opened a school in New York. At about that time Albers settled at Black Mountain College in North Carolina, a relatively out-of-the-way place but one that soon drew a talented group of students and other teachers like Willem de Kooning, Franz Kline and Robert Motherwell, whose names became outstanding in American art in subsequent years.

Hofmann brought to the teaching of painting an extremely varied and valuable background. Born in 1880, he became a close friend of Picasso, Braque, Matisse, Delaunay and other modernists as a student in Paris at the turn of the century. There, he was in consequence present at the birth of the two most vital and revolutionary innovations of 20th Century art—Cubism and Fauvism.

Cubism, with its emphasis on forms, and Fauvism, based on a vivid expressiveness of color, found integration in Hofmann's paintings. The ideas that he expressed in his work and in his teachings had tremendous influence in America, not only upon his own students, but on those who had a chance to see his work at exhibitions in New York and at the artist's retreat of Provincetown, Massachusetts, where Hofmann

New York became the home in exile for a remarkable group of artists who were forced by the war to leave Europe. Continuing their careers in New York, they painted, exhibited and met often. One of the galleries that put on shows of their work was run by Pierre Matisse, a son of the great French master. This photograph was made in the Matisse gallery in March 1942. It shows, in the first row from left to right, the Chilean-born painter Matta, sculptor Ossip Zadkine, the Surrealist leaders Yves Tanguy and Max Ernst, the fantasist Marc Chagall and the French Cubist master Fernand Léger. In the second row are Surrealism's poet-philosopher André Breton, the Dutchman Piet Mondrian, painters André Masson and Amédée Ozenfant, sculptor Jacques Lipchitz and painter Eugene Berman. Standing in the rear are Surrealists Pavel Tchelitchew and Kurt Seligmann.

ran a summer school. Hofmann's presence in America provided a powerful impetus for artists interested in abstraction, which had become somewhat out of fashion amid the popularity of the Social Realism of the Depression years. To painters who insisted that art be used in the service of humanitarian causes—a difficult assertion to challenge, particularly in that difficult period—the philosophy of Art for Art's Sake seemed selfish and effete. Nevertheless, in its simplest form, that was the doctrine that Hofmann's teaching upheld. He insisted that painting was, first and foremost, an esthetic experience. To force it to serve any other master was to corrupt it.

Hofmann was an ideal spokesman for this position. He had undergone one of the most complete educations in abstract art that it was possible to acquire. His theory of painting was based on the assertion, familiar from the time of Cézanne, that before being anything else a painting was an arrangement of colors and forms on a two-dimensional surface. Added to this was his formulation of a principle he called "push and pull"—a tension between the flat surface of the canvas and the sense of depth, or third dimension, evoked by the elements of color and form that the painter places upon that surface. "Depth," he stated, "in a pictorial, plastic sense is not created by the arrangement of objects one after another toward a vanishing point, in the sense of the Renaissance perspective, but on the contrary (and in absolute denial of this doctrine) by the creation of forces in the sense of *push* and *pull*."

This difficult concept becomes clearer through an examination of Hofmann's own paintings *(page 125)*. It is apparent that some of his colors advance and others recede, some forms appear to lie behind others, some textures create hills, some valleys. Each element, moreover, is opposed by a countering element. While everything thus inevitably remains on the picture surface, everything is nevertheless moving, or appearing to move, back and forth within the picture plane. Depth is created out of this tension.

Hofmann was also aware of the force that an evolving painting exerts on its own creator. Since the abstract artist was not beginning with an image that he wanted to record, in a representational sense, he was to some extent controlled by what he did on the canvas. Each line and color he placed on the surface affected the eventual painting in a way that the artist could not predict. This circumstance of being dictated to by the painting in process emphasized the difficult position of the contemporary abstractionist. Working neither from a sketch nor directly from nature, the artist engages in a constant dialogue with himself. But the self that responds from the canvas, as soon as it is visible there, already has an objective reality; the process is not, therefore, simply a private, internal experience. This give-and-take between the artist and his work was to assume increasing importance in the movement spawned by the generation of painters who came of age in the years between the wars.

Albers, like Hofmann, was concerned with color, but delved deeply into its properties and its perception by the eye and mind of the observer. First in his work at Black Mountain and later at Yale, he presented the potentialities of color in ways that many artists had never considered. In his monumental work, *Interaction of Color,* a treatise based on his teaching program, Albers demonstrated hundreds of ways in which a color changes its character in juxtaposition to a neighboring color, an opposite color or a related color. He showed opaque colors demonstrating translucency, warm colors revealing coolness and intense colors losing their identity altogether. In his own paintings *(page 182),* Albers adopted a geometrical motif of squares within squares to limit the formal ideas in his work and let the exploration of color interactions come through. Regarded by many as cold, mechanical and lifeless, Albers' paintings nevertheless have a character that no careful observer can fail to respond to.

Hitler's Nazi regime had driven both Hofmann and Albers to America. The arrival of World War II led many other artists to follow, and forced the return to the United States of a number of American painters who had been living, studying and working abroad. Among the foreign artists who came to America were the French Cubist painter Fernand Léger, whose interest in the forms of the technological age was expressed in elegantly designed canvases, and the Purist Jean Helion, whose work is today little known but whose propagandizing on behalf of abstract art did much to widen the audience for abstractionism. Finally, in 1940, the Dutchman Piet Mondrian arrived in New York, preceded by a formidable reputation.

Mondrian's presence in New York was an important one. Of all the painters who used Cubism as a starting point he, more than most, showed how the style could be manipulated in a wholly original direction. Almost all other artists experimenting with Cubist techniques had been so enthralled by Picasso's and Braque's original variants on their own styles that the works they turned out were frankly imitative. Mondrian found a way out of the dilemma by pioneering a rigorous but provocative style that ultimately became known as Neo-Plasticism. Totally committing himself to a fully abstract manner, Mondrian based the formal structure of his Neo-Plastic paintings on the right angle, which does not exist in nature; he further adopted a limited range of color, mostly employing black and white with flat rectangular areas of red, yellow or blue.

The upheavals of war in Europe also brought to America a group of artists whose aims and styles could not have been more different from those of Hofmann, Albers and Mondrian. These were the followers of Surrealism, a movement almost two decades old. It came to New York in a rush in 1941 with the almost simultaneous arrival of Max Ernst, André Masson and André Breton, the latter not a painter but a writer and poet and the man who became the spokesman and virtual dictator of the Surrealist style.

The Surrealist technique explored the dreamlike mental states and images latent in the mind. This fantasy world was further sparked by artistic surprises and unlikely juxtapositions of objects, such as a swarm of ants on a pocket watch. Considerably influenced by Freud, the Surrealists took over man's hidden mental processes as a suitable and fruitful area of exploration in art. Delving into their own psyches and relying on the pressure of unconscious forces to create their art, the Surrealist painters and poets provided a whole new battery of methods and imagery.

Surrealist style had been known in the United States before the 1940s, but only when the masters themselves arrived did American artists obtain firsthand knowledge of it. Breton, the handsome, leonine-featured leader of the group, was a commanding presence and an articulate proselytizer. As important as Breton were Yves Tanguy, Ernst and Masson. The flamboyant and unpredictable Spanish Surrealist Salvador Dali, who had arrived in the United States in 1940, also attracted a great deal of attention to the Surrealist style. His personal manner—he was an unabashed publicity hound, social climber and entrepreneur—tended to make serious artists a bit suspicious of him. Nevertheless, Dali's paintings, with their limp watches and grotesque, disembodied figures introduced a fascinating world that gallerygoers had never seen before.

Most of the Surrealists came to public attention through the efforts of a dynamic and eccentric woman named Peggy Guggenheim, heiress to a healthy portion of her family's mining fortune. Miss Guggenheim —known that way despite several marriages—for years had lived an expatriate life in Europe, but returned with most other Americans when the war seemed inevitable. She brought with her an enormous entourage, as she herself noted: "We were eleven people: one husband, two ex-wives, one future husband and seven children." She was also accompanied by a treasury of books, drawings and paintings that she had been collecting for some years and that she had used to stock an art gallery in London.

The gallery, called Guggenheim Jeune, had been started as much for a lark as anything else, but its founder became increasingly serious and sophisticated about contemporary art. Her first guide, in fact, was one of the great innovators of art in this century, Marcel Duchamp. Duchamp taught Miss Guggenheim to distinguish between abstract and Surrealist art and introduced her to many bright talents, including Jean Arp and Jean Cocteau, whose one-man show, hung by Duchamp, had opened the gallery in 1937. She also showed the Russian abstractionist Wassily Kandinsky, who had been at the Bauhaus in Germany with Albers. Others she knew and exhibited were the sculptors Brancusi and Alexander Calder. Two of the most interesting and devoted Surrealist painters Miss Guggenheim began collecting were also two men with whom she had love affairs—Tanguy and Ernst. She later married Ernst and brought him to the United States in that curious planeload of baggage, lovers and art.

Ernst, more than any other artist, experimented with Surrealist techniques. He invented such devices as "frottage" (literally, rub), which involved rubbing the surface of a textured object like a rough piece of driftwood with a lead pencil and then rubbing a blank canvas over its surface to pick up the texture. Another Ernst device was called "decalcomania," a method in which two canvases that had been crudely slathered with paint were pressed together and then pulled apart. The resulting patterns, which looked something like Rorschach ink blots, were used as starting points for paintings.

The basic idea behind these techniques, which at first might sound frivolous, was that the painter could free himself from preconceptions of what a painting should be in order to concentrate on the process of painting itself. Digging deeply into his unconscious, he could respond not to nature or to some thematic or literary idea, but to the painting itself as a complete and living thing—much in the manner described by Hofmann. Sometimes playful and capricious, sometimes angry or even savage, the artist's mood during the act of creation became the principal determinant of not only the look but the character of his work.

Along with new techniques and the concept of freeing the artist's unconscious, American art seized upon other ideas from abroad in the '30s and '40s. One of the most important was Oriental philosophy. Western artists had long been fascinated by Eastern art; Whistler and the French Impressionist Manet had been much influenced by Japanese woodcuts and Chinese scroll painting and porcelain design. But their interest was essentially in the new forms they saw—the flat areas of color, the delicate line and subtle harmony of composition. The Oriental influence on American art was to be far subtler and deeper. One of the first Americans to incorporate Oriental thinking into his paintings was Mark Tobey (page 130). Curiously, the techniques of Zen Buddhism, which Tobey learned while studying in Japan in 1934, parallel those of Surrealism. Both try to penetrate the mind to clear away the rational processes and get at the inner recesses of experience.

Tobey spent much of his time in Seattle, where he became the leader of the so-called Pacific Northwest Painters, a group that included Morris Graves (page 131). New York City, however, was the capital of experimental activity in the arts. Most of the artists, dealers and patrons lived in Manhattan, and the major museums and collections dedicated to modern art were founded there. Alfred Stieglitz had led the way in the early decades of the century with his "291" Gallery, and he continued in the late 1920s with the Intimate Gallery. Early in the '20s the patroness Katherine Dreier, with the help of Marcel Duchamp, organized what they called the Société Anonyme to promote avant-garde art and artists. Later in the same decade the wealthy patron Albert Gallatin, a painter himself, established the Museum of Living Art at New York University, where for some 15 years students and painters could view a collection of works by the leading European and American experimentalists. In 1929 the Museum of Modern Art was established in a small suite of rooms on the 12th floor of a midtown skyscraper; it moved into its own modern building on West 53rd Street in 1939. The Whitney Museum of American Art came into existence in 1930, displaying as part of its first exhibit the exquisite collection of Gertrude Vanderbilt Whitney, who had been a devotee of art even before she served as a sponsor of the Armory Show in 1913. In the same year that the Museum of Modern Art found its permanent home, Solomon Guggenheim opened the Museum of Non-Objective Art, which later became known simply as the "Guggenheim" when it moved into a handsome new headquarters on Fifth Avenue designed by Frank Lloyd Wright. Not to be outdone by her uncle, Peggy Guggenheim in 1942 established a combination gallery and museum, which she called Art of This Century.

Yet in America at large, and even at the New York fountainhead, interest in modern art in the '30s and '40s was confined primarily to avant-garde patrons, a few discerning art critics and curators, and the artists themselves. Abstraction was still beyond the ken of most Americans. To rectify the situation, in 1936 a group of artists formed an association called The American Abstract Artists to bring their works before a wider audience, promote public appreciation and "afford each artist the opportunity of developing his own work by becoming familiar with the efforts of others." The association held yearly exhibitions, sponsored workshops and seminars, and published books, but their efforts were only partly successful; even when modern works were sold in America for sizable sums, their creators remained largely unrecognized by the general public.

This shadow of obscurity hung over many of America's best artists. One of these was Arshile Gorky, a tragic figure who, without realizing it, became the most important link between the abstractionists of that period and those of later decades. An Armenian, Gorky had come to the United States in 1920 at the age of 16. After his arrival, he studied art in Providence and Boston, haunting the museums in his spare time, earning his meals washing dishes. Money was a lifelong problem for Gorky; even after he had earned some critical attention and sold a few paintings he was seldom free from financial worry.

Gorky's evolution as a painter is typical of that of most young American artists in the first half of the 20th Century. He began by responding to Cézanne, whose innovations in both form and color had by the 1920s become the classical foundations of the new abstract art. Gradually he worked his way through the styles of other modern masters. As a result, his work often seemed derivative to buyers and critics, and his imitative habits perhaps contributed to his failure to achieve early success. But he was learning, building up a repertoire of ideas and forms that were eventually released in a personal style.

What finally freed Gorky was Surrealism. With its emphasis on myth and dream and the life of the unconscious, the style and its techniques awakened in him a long-dormant response to the legends of his Armenian boyhood and the vivid memories he retained of his native country. In the early 1940s Gorky finally brought all the elements of his style together. He married for the second time in 1941 and his new wife, a Boston girl named Agnes Magruder, bore his first child, a girl, in 1943. Perhaps the stability of a home life enabled him to find himself, for he was a deeply affectionate man and full of bright optimism in the early stages of his marriage. His art grew as his family did. He returned to nature for inspiration and painted fully abstract but lyrical canvases with such titles as *The Plow and the Song* and *Water of the Flowery Mill.* But Gorky's years of fulfillment were short. At the peak of his creative powers a series of misfortunes befell him. In 1945, the last good thing that happened to him—aside from the developing greatness of his work *(pages 116, 133-135)*—was the birth of a second daughter.

In January 1946 a fire in Gorky's Connecticut studio destroyed almost 30 paintings and dozens of drawings and sketches—virtually all of his output over the previous year, plus some pictures he had been working on for several years. Among these were several portraits of his wife. Only a few weeks after the fire Gorky was hospitalized, to be operated on for cancer. The operation was apparently successful, but it took a tremendous toll of his energy and confidence. Always a vigorous man, he deeply felt the loss of health. His depression was aggravated by profound frustration over the destruction of his work.

Gorky briefly bounced back the following year, part of which he spent at a farm in Virginia owned by his wife's family. There he made a series of powerful ink and watercolor drawings incorporating the light of a fireplace with furniture and elements of the human figure. Evidently obsessed with these symbols of love, hearth and home, he was evolving forms and ideas that would emerge in his last great paintings. Some successes in museum shows and galleries followed, and Gorky turned out work at a furious pace. Perhaps he sensed that time was running out.

In June 1948 misfortune caught up with Gorky once more: he broke his neck in an automobile accident. Although he received every assurance that he would completely recover he suffered an intensely uncomfortable convalescence. Beyond that, his marriage was beginning to fail. Finally, Gorky's wife left him, apparently because she was concerned about the effect of the disintegrating marriage on their two young children, whom she took with her. On the telephone several days later she offered to return, but Gorky evidently refused. The next day he hanged himself.

It has been argued that Gorky was the last of the Surrealist painters and the first of the Abstract Expressionists, the movement initiated by Jackson Pollock just before Gorky's death. But no label is sufficient to encompass his vision or define his place. His longtime friend and former student Ethel Schwabacher wrote in her definitive biography that "he used a contemporary structure, cubism, and a contemporary method, the automatism of surrealism; he also used . . . the psychology of the unconscious. But for his imagery he drew on his early life or his sensations of nature. . . . Gorky's map might be the fields of Connecticut or Virginia; his myth, the poetry of sex. The artist was as concerned with this vast hidden world seen by the mind alone as with the scarcely more accessible world seen by the eyes."

Gorky propelled American art into the postwar decades. He had merged the Surrealists' ideas with imagery and techniques adopted from the Cubists and Picasso. The forms of abstraction that he sowed would provide rich harvests of painting in the late 1940s and early 1950s—when a truly original American style would be seen at last.

Hans Hofmann: *The Cliff*, c. 1961

# Experiments in Abstraction

European ideas about abstract art were a strong stimulus to American painting during the 1930s and 1940s. They appeared not only in the form of works exhibited at museums and galleries but also in the personal teaching of men like Hans Hofmann, a distinguished German-born painter who had experimented with almost every form of modern art. Hofmann's painting above is a forceful example of his theory of "push-pull," a nonobjective work that derives its impact from intense, gemlike colors contrasted with matte blacks, and from bold, thickly textured strokes opposed by delicate, driplike swirls.

Burgoyne Diller: *Second Theme #21*, 1944-1946

Following the lead of the Dutch painter Piet Mondrian, who spent the last four years of his life in New York, Burgoyne Diller and Fritz Glarner probed the possibilities of Geometric Abstraction. Diller had studied with Hofmann, who in 1933 praised him as America's most promising painter. But Diller's own ideas led him to a style that sometimes came strikingly close to Mondrian's in its use of primary colors, right angles and asymmetric compositions.

Fritz Glarner interpreted Mondrian more freely. In

Fritz Glarner: *Relational Painting*, 1949-1951

the painting above he used a motif of lines and primary colors, but transformed rectangles into wedgelike shapes and arranged them in overlapping and interlocking planes. Glarner, who produced a 40-by-15-foot mural of similar patterns for the lobby of an office building in New York City, called his works "relational paintings." Like other Geometric Abstractionists he believed that his art, despite its apparent obsession with mathematical forms, had a profound relation to the tension and emotion of life.

127

Two major influences—Surrealism and Cubism—are at work in Bradley Walker Tomlin's painting at right. Seemingly incompatible, the two styles are here blended by Tomlin into a compelling whole: the ghostly Surrealist head of a mannequin is placed with great care among the Cubistically treated objects of a still life —a table, a glass and flowers. Tomlin's unabashed melding of styles is characteristically American; a European artist, committed to the idea that a style is a style and not to be tampered with, would not have attempted such a thing. But, freed by distance and temperament, the American could dare—and succeed.

Tomlin's eclectic blending of ideas was only a way station in his artistic career. He remained an experimenter until his death in 1953, concerned that he might be locked into only one mode: "Does the artist find that the seemingly effortless structure, which he has evolved with total clarity, tends on repetition to escape him? That in spite of the production of masterpieces, art itself remains infinitely mysterious and that the work in progress is merely a kind of hall rack on which he has hung various nicely woven articles of clothing; jackets shabbily elegant, old hats battered to his image? Confronted by the cast of his own mind, he says, it is at least mine. Yet the jacket he has slipped into binds slightly under the armpits. Umbrellas and old walking sticks clatter to the floor."

Bradley Walker Tomlin: *Still Life*, 1939

Mark Tobey: *New Life (Resurrection)*, 1957

As artists on the East Coast of the United States have been influenced by art currents from Europe, those on the West Coast have felt the spirit of the Orient. Both Mark Tobey and Morris Graves, who spent much of their painting careers in the Northwest, traveled and studied in China and Japan. While their work is very different, both share elements of Oriental philosophy and, in some cases, the pictorial style of the Far East.

Tobey, born in Wisconsin, traveled widely in Europe and the Middle East before settling in Seattle. In 1934 he studied Chinese calligraphy in Shanghai and then retired briefly to a Zen Buddhist monastery at Kyoto, in Japan. There, as he tells it, the monks gave him a piece of paper with a big zero drawn on it and told him to meditate. The story may be apocryphal; in any event Tobey began to employ calligraphic techniques in his painting, often reversing the traditional tones to use white brushstrokes on dark backgrounds. "I used to paint shapes," he once said, "now I write lines. To me, the dynamic line is what matters."

In 1951, the year of his first retrospective exhibit, Tobey indicated that his "white writing," as he called it, was a rejection of Cubism. "Art," he said, "has to express the rhythm of life, the dancing motion. Painting can't be bound to cubes and solids." He insisted that Cézanne, despite an avowed dedication to cubes and solids, eventually reached for the same quality: "In Cézanne's last work, you no longer saw a house, but a movement of a brush." A mystic and a member of the Bahai faith, an attempted fusion of the teachings of all religions, Tobey tried to express his reactions to forces at work in the world. In his painting at the left, the gray masses symbolize "old earth, before and upon which dance the elemental figurations of new life."

Morris Graves became similarly preoccupied with symbols and mystical perceptions, but he expressed himself in more concrete images. His *Bird in the Spirit (below)* is one of a series of paintings in which he used birds as private emblems. Tantalizing and mysterious, Graves's birds mean various things to various observers. Graves himself identified his aim in art only as making notations about the external world "with which to verify the inner eye."

Morris Graves: *Bird in the Spirit,* 1940-1941

Milton Avery: *Mother and Child*, 1944

Matisse and Picasso have left indelible marks on the art of their time, not least in America. In these two paintings, Milton Avery and Arshile Gorky show their debts to the masters. Above, Avery adopts the fluid contours and flat forms of Matisse, but chooses his own distinctive colors and paints in thin veils.

Gorky's monumental forms *(right)* echo the early Picasso. Gorky, however, was uncomfortable trying to assimilate the style of others into his own work; he worked on this picture for years without ever completing it to his own satisfaction. In his later paintings *(overleaf)* he found his own style.

Arshile Gorky: *The Artist and His Mother*, 1926-1929

133

Gorky distilled from Surrealism a way to express
his innermost feelings. He appears to confront his
deepest anxieties in these two paintings from his last
year of active work. Their creation was preceded by a
series of tragedies—a studio fire that destroyed much
of his work, an operation for cancer, the beginning of
the breakup of his marriage. In the work below, he
drew upon a traditional image of death, a faceless
rider astride a phantom horse. But the title, *Betrothal*,
and the warm accents of lavender and red suggest a
duality: love seems coupled with death. Love and
sexual imagery are also latent in *Agony (right)*, a
painting done in the same year and based on sketches
Gorky had made of the fireplace in his wife's family
home. Forms that evoke many things—a crib, a chair,
a hearth, flower petals—combine with colors
suggestive of flame, passion, emptiness. Yet while such
images may be present, the interpretation, as with all
abstract art, is in the end up to the viewer himself.

Arshile Gorky: *Betrothal, II*, 1947

Arshile Gorky: *Agony,* 1948

# VI

# Birth of
# a Native Style

In *Moon Woman Cuts the
Circle* Jackson Pollock shows
a mythical matriarchal figure,
perhaps derived from Mexican
art or American Indian legend,
slashing with her knife a black
circle in a night-blue
background. Characteristic of
Pollock's early interest in
dreamlike imagery, the
painting also shows the violent
thrusts and counterthrusts that
became the mark of his later,
fully abstract works.

Jackson Pollock: *Moon
Woman Cuts the Circle,* 1944-1945

After World War II, American artists took the lead in establishing an
original and powerful style that soon came to dominate the art world.
Called Abstract Expressionism, it grew out of a number of influences,
but in the end was a uniquely American product. It was also probably
the last style that could be described as native to any country, for the
postwar boom in global communications created a genuine internationalism in the arts. As Jackson Pollock, the first great innovator of
postwar American painting, once said: "An American is an American
and his painting would naturally be qualified by that fact, whether he
wills it or not. But the basic problems of contemporary painting are independent of any one country."

Nevertheless, America did make a singular contribution to the history of painting in the late 1940s and 1950s. In his huge canvases, covered with swirls and drips of paint from edge to edge, Pollock found
the syntax for a wholly new kind of painting. Essentially nonobjective, with no subject matter other than what the viewer saw before him
—paint on canvas—the new works were resolutely individualistic. No
longer bound to European influences, the American artist struck out
on his own, employing new materials—synthetic paints, unprimed canvas—and avoiding elegant brushwork or any traditional marks of the
artist's "hand." Most of all, these new works insisted that the artist's
personal expression should be his primary concern. Sometimes highly
emotional, sometimes highly intellectual, the new abstract art dared to
stand on its own merits without the support of an older tradition and
with only the force of the artist's integrity and will to sustain it.

It is quite fitting that Pollock should have been the leader in the
U.S. contribution to art. Too much has been made of it, but the fact
that Pollock was born in Cody, Wyoming, lends a certain authenticity,
as well as a healthy dollop of romance, to the oft-advanced claims that
his work was truly American. Wide-open spaces, the speed of travel
possible on ruler-straight Western highways, an exposure to Indian
art and legend, an intimate acquaintance with great natural wonders
like the desert, the Rocky Mountains and the Grand Canyon—all add-

ed up to distinctive influences on a painter who was to acquire considerable sophistication, but who was first and foremost an American country boy.

Pollock's parents were born and raised in Iowa, but were living in Cody when, on January 28, 1912, Jackson—the fifth son—was born. LeRoy, the father, tried for the next several years to support his family as a farmer but, moving between Wyoming, Arizona and California, he never quite made a go of it. When Jackson was 10, his eldest brother, Charles, left home and got a job on a newspaper while he studied art. It was perhaps his influence that led his youngest brother in the same direction. In 1926 Charles went to New York to study at the Art Students League with Thomas Hart Benton, who later became Jackson's friend and teacher. Two of the other Pollock brothers, Marvin Jay and Sanford, also studied art and later worked in the printing and graphic-arts fields. But for many years it was Charles's example, and the books and magazines that he sent to Jackson, that helped form the younger man's thinking and kept his enthusiasm for art alive.

Jackson's first exposure to formal art classes took place in Los Angeles, where he studied at Manual Arts High School with a stimulating teacher named Frederick Schwankovsky. Beginning in earnest to draw and paint and model in clay, Pollock was nevertheless a rebellious student and was twice expelled. The second expulsion, in 1929, marked the end of Pollock's formal education. But his wide reading, partly directed at long distance by his brother Charles, gave him a broad acquaintance with literature, politics and philosophy.

During several summers in his teen-age years, Pollock worked with his father and brothers in land-surveying jobs in Arizona and California. The work gave him an intimate knowledge of the open spaces of the Southwest, its Indian legends, its tortured geological features, and its distinctive plant and animal life. But his association with the hard-drinking survey crews and workmen may have been a factor in a problem that was to plague him all his life. In these youthful years Pollock became an alcoholic. For most of his adult life he tried to rid himself of the problem through psychoanalysis and chemotherapy, but he never fully succeeded.

Pollock's serious art studies began in 1930, when he came to New York City to enroll in classes at the Art Students League under Benton, his brother's mentor. The work of the American Scene painter and muralist constituted the first strong influence on Pollock's art—one which introduced him, among other things, to Renaissance forms and the energy and movement of heroic figures. Benton's mural commissions gave Pollock a chance to see such large-scale work in progress, and he in fact posed for some of the figures in them. Benton took Pollock under his wing and for the next five years or so provided the younger man with continuous encouragement and support. In 1935 Benton wrote Pollock: "Before I get started on my own stuff and forget everything else I want to tell you I think the little sketches you left around here are magnificent. Your color is rich and beautiful. You've the stuff, old kid—all you have to do is keep it up."

Although Benton and Pollock remained on good terms for many years, Pollock increasingly moved away from his teacher's romantic realism. "My work with Benton," he once said, "was important as something against which to react very strongly, later on; in this it was better to have worked with him than with a less resistant personality who would have provided a much less strong opposition." He was "damn grateful to Tom," Pollock declared. "He drove his kind of realism at me so hard I bounced right into nonobjective painting."

Pollock's style evolved slowly in New York, where he settled down to live with his brother Sanford, also a budding artist. Living on the relief program of the New Deal, the two brothers shared an apartment in Greenwich Village where, in the bars, the lofts and studios of many artists, the new styles were argued and developed. Like Paris in the late 19th Century, New York was the focus of a band of enormously talented men bursting with ideas and energy, consumed with a passion to speak their minds and project their visions, each in his own fashion. The importance of this community of artistic spirits cannot be underestimated; out of the cauldron of their discussions rose the ideas and inspirations for the coming breakthrough of American art. Not least important was the feeling of each man that he was among friends; with the traditional art world almost unanimously hostile to new forms of art, these sensitive individuals needed a place where they did not feel like outcasts.

Society at large did not have much to offer Pollock in these years, except the humiliating relief checks. But finally some of the programs set up under Franklin Roosevelt provided a more dignified way for him to earn a living. From 1935 to 1943 Pollock worked off and on with the Federal Art Project of the Works Progress Administration. He was required to submit a painting every eight weeks, presumably for allocation to some government office or public building around the country. In all, Pollock painted about 50 works for the Project, but almost all of them have mysteriously disappeared. His arrangement with the Project was an undemanding one, however, and in the hours when he was not working on easel paintings he was fortunate enough to take part in a mural workshop in New York led by the great Mexican artist David Siqueiros.

Siqueiros proved an important influence on Pollock's later style, introducing him to many of the methods and materials that he later employed. Perhaps most importantly, the Mexican muralist was working on a large scale. In addition, he was experimenting with air guns that sprayed paint, with drip and splatter techniques, and with synthetic paints and commercial lacquers of brilliant color and high gloss. He used many of these fast-drying, bright materials on banners and floats that he decorated for Communist demonstrations in New York and elsewhere. Like many intellectuals and artists of the 1930s, Pollock flirted with Communism, but he soon dropped his interest in the movement. The spirit of experimentation in the Siqueiros workshop, however, was an invaluable artistic experience for him.

In 1937 Pollock began psychiatric treatment in an effort to cure his

One of the few paintings by Jackson Pollock that survive from his years with the Federal Art Project during the Depression is this gloomy landscape, which shows flamelike forms erupting from the tops of a group of factory buildings. Pollock received about $100 a month for his work for the federal agency and was expected to produce one painting every eight weeks or so. Under similar arrangements, some 5,000 artists created 108,000 paintings, 18,800 sculptures, 11,300 original prints and 2,500 murals for public buildings.

drinking problem. He continued treatments for years, but with only limited success. One important side effect was that Pollock became involved with an analyst who used the artist's own drawings and sketches as a way of reaching Pollock's unconscious anxieties. The analyst was a follower of Carl Jung, the Swiss psychiatrist who was one of the founders of modern psychoanalysis. Unlike Freud, Jung placed great emphasis on the importance of myths, symbols and legends to the unconscious workings of the human mind. This contact with Jungian ideas had a profound effect on Pollock's art. Works of the early 1940s like *The She-Wolf, Pasiphaë, Male and Female* and *The Moon Woman Cuts the Circle (page 136)* contain a great deal of symbolism and mystical overtones.

During this period, Pollock was exposed to the ideas of Surrealism by the American painter Robert Motherwell, and he responded enthusiastically. Surrealism's ideas and techniques closely paralleled those he had been formulating. The notion of delving into the unconscious, of using materials from dreams or mystical legends, had become part of his repertoire. But one of the things that had been missing from his personal type of Surrealism was the technique of automatism. Automatism suggests that the artist allow his hand to wander freely across the surface of his canvas or paper, permitting himself to be directed by inner impulses as much as possible. Like the exploration of ancient myths and symbols, automatism was an attempt to express profound and basic human emotions through the experience and sensibilities of the individual artist. Pollock and his contemporaries, each in his own way, sought to achieve this goal.

In 1943 Pollock had a stroke of luck. He met Peggy Guggenheim, patroness extraordinary of modern art. Miss Guggenheim exhibited some of Pollock's work in her Art of This Century gallery and then offered him a contract guaranteeing him $150 a month. While not exactly a bonanza, the money was sufficient to free Pollock to paint full time. Two years later she increased the stipend to $300—in return for his total artistic output—and also lent him money for a down payment on a house in Springs, Long Island, near the summer resort of East Hampton. Shortly after buying the house, Pollock married Lee Krasner, a young painter he had known for some years. Lee had studied painting with Hans Hofmann and was to continue to paint throughout her married life, sometimes exhibiting with Jackson in group shows. She also proved a steady source of encouragement and support. This was vital to Pollock, who fluctuated between supreme confidence and profound uncertainty about his work. Mrs. Pollock once recalled standing in front of one of her husband's recently completed canvases, which she thought was very good, and hearing him ask, " 'Is this a painting?' Not is this a good painting or a bad one, but a *painting!*"

In addition to exhibiting his work and providing him with a small but steady income, Peggy Guggenheim commissioned Pollock to paint a mural for her town house on 61st Street in New York. On the advice of Marcel Duchamp, Miss Guggenheim's friend and adviser, Pollock painted the mural on canvas so that it could be done in his studio and later moved to her house. The chance to work on a large scale was a decisive turn of events for Pollock and he seemed to sense it. He was filled with anxiety over the work. After ripping out a wall in his studio to accommodate the giant canvas, he sat in front of it, as Peggy Guggenheim recalled, "completely uninspired for days, getting more and more depressed." Finally, he painted it all in one session. Almost 8 feet tall and 20 feet long, it consisted of a band of rhythmic swirls and shapes in blue, white and yellow. Over the freely brushed surface, he dripped black paint. Hung in the entrance hall of Miss Guggenheim's house, the mural pulsed with energy that reached out to cover every part of its surface with dramatic movement and color. Thereafter, Pollock's canvases became larger and larger, until virtually all of his works were of mural size. The direction was right for him. His background as a Westerner and his appreciation of what he called the West's "vast horizontality," his work in the Siqueiros mural workshop, his own assertive personality—all added up to a personal expression of expansiveness.

Peggy Guggenheim's Art of This Century gallery not only gave Pollock a chance to be seen by the public; it introduced him to a group of artists, both American and European, whose ideas he found tremendously stimulating. Among the young New York artists with whom he exhibited were Motherwell and William Baziotes, Clyfford Still, Mark Rothko, Adolph Gottlieb and Ad Reinhardt.

The work of each of these men was distinctly different, but all of them were finding that to a considerable degree their problems and the solutions they sought were similar. First of all, they had to confront the fabulous creative force of Picasso—the giant of the times, an inventor and destroyer of styles, and a prodigious workman. From Cubism to Surrealism, from landscape to still life, from portrait to figure study, Picasso had done it all. In his variations on the linear treatment of the human body, Picasso had invented a whole encyclopedia of new forms; in his assimilation of the raw power of primitive art he had found expression for deep, underlying emotions that concretely related to modern times. It was clear to the young Americans that the almost overwhelming influence of Picasso had to be surmounted. (Lee Pollock once heard a crash in the next room and heard Jackson shout: "God damn it, that guy missed nothing!" She discovered that he had thrown a book of Picasso reproductions to the floor.)

Other strong forces were contributing to the collective dilemma in which Pollock and his fellow artists found themselves. Wassily Kandinsky's early nonobjective paintings were now almost 40 years old but the impact of their newness had not worn off. Paul Klee's magical, cipher-filled little abstractions also had to be reckoned with. Miró's fantasy world of floating shapes and colors had an even more stunning effect on the American moderns. In contrast to past eras, in which one style was dominant and painters could react more or less consistently to a body of work cast in a single vein, the mid-1940s were a confusing, disorienting time. American abstract painters were faced with too many choices; too many possibilities were open.

Photographed from the loft of his barnlike studio on Long Island, Jackson Pollock *(above)* squats beside one of his large paint-splattered canvases and selects a color from an array of opened cans of the commercial enamels and automobile lacquers he preferred. Below, he drips sand onto the surface of a painting, a technique he used to create especially thick textures.

Willem de Kooning, one of the foremost American painters to come out of the period, later said that it was Pollock who broke the ice. Harold Rosenberg, the articulate and influential art critic who perhaps best encapsulated the style of the moment, calling it "action painting," wrote: "At a certain moment the canvas began to appear to one American painter after another as an arena in which to act—rather than as a space in which to reproduce, redesign, analyze or 'express' an object, actual or imagined. What was to go on the canvas was not a picture but an event. The painter no longer approached his easel with an image in his mind; he went up to it with material in his hand to do something to that other piece of material in front of him. The image would be the result of this encounter."

How did Pollock arrive at this breakthrough? First of all, he had long been concerned with the future of easel painting, believing that it had outlived its effectiveness. In an application for a foundation grant in 1947, Pollock declared that his aim was to create a new form of painting somewhere between easel size and mural size, as a prelude to a truly acceptable wall-filling style of painting. The mural that he was commissioned to paint for Peggy Guggenheim's New York town house was a preliminary step in this direction.

This chance to work on a really large scale had been for Pollock a stimulating experience, but it was not until 1947 that he really opened up his style and produced something entirely new. It was then that he began fully to abandon traditional techniques, to place his unprimed, unstretched canvas on the floor and drip, splatter and swirl paints on it. Here, suddenly, was what he had been searching for. Concerned no longer with a preconceived imagery, Pollock now, as he put it, got "in" the painting, creating as he went. Responding directly to the flow of paint, he combined the automatic Surrealist techniques with the controlled sensibilities of the experienced draftsman and colorist to produce works unlike anything seen before. In the best of them, Pollock rigorously avoided delineating any formal pattern or arrangement. It must have taken extraordinary control for him to reject even the natural rhythm of his arm as it moved across the surface of his canvases, tracing the sprawling, linear flow of paint that seemed at times to come right out of his innards. Treating the whole canvas with equal attention, not permitting himself to turn back in his painting process or linger on any focal point, Pollock created huge compositions that confront the viewer with their forthrightness, and envelop him in a web of visual sensation, emotion and mystery.

Pollock's paintings were described by one early critic as having "an air of baked macaroni." They were more correctly identified by another as an attempt "to express feeling that ranges from pleasant enthusiasm through wildness to explosiveness, as purely and as well as possible"—an aim widely shared in the artistic climate of New York in the late 1940s. In time the efforts to achieve that goal—the expression of the individual artist's feeling—came to be the movement called Abstract Expressionism.

Among the other first-rate painters who were involved in the movement, sometimes referred to as the New York School, were de Kooning and Franz Kline, both friends of Pollock. De Kooning, a Dutch-born artist, had originally been trained as a house painter—a craft that, in his day, required the ability to simulate wood textures and marble patterns and to produce a subtle range of colors. De Kooning had been introduced as a young man to the austere geometric school called *de Stijl*, whose members included his countryman Piet Mondrian. But in his evolving style de Kooning combined an interest in landscape and the human figure with extraordinarily bold and evocative abstractions, sometimes in disorienting cosmetic tones of pale yellow, pink and buff *(page 151)*. In a series entitled "Women" de Kooning attacked the canvas with a savage brush, sometimes letting the paint drip and dribble down the surface *(page 150)*. Also influenced by the Surrealists, and his good friend Arshile Gorky, de Kooning regards these accidental drips and splatters as natural accidents that sometimes add another dimension to his work.

De Kooning's work often reveals a sensuality and elegance that perhaps derive from his European background. In contrast, Kline, who was born in an eastern Pennsylvania mining town, brings to his painting *(pages 148-149)* a raw vitality and boldness that seem characteristically American. Kline reached his maturity with a long series of black-and-white paintings in which the principal imagery consists of broad, slashing strokes that set up strong tensions on the surface of the canvas. Virtually crashing out of the frame, these images produce sensations akin both to the boldness of Oriental calligraphy and to the sweep of suspension bridges. Kline eventually reintroduced color in his work, but the vitality remained.

Other key members of the New York School included Philip Guston and Clyfford Still, whose abstractions are full of tactile sensation, a feeling for the texture of paint on canvas. More carefully structured is the work of Gottlieb and Motherwell, whose imagery tends toward variations on geometric and symbolic shapes. There are in addition men who moved dramatically away from Pollock, like the brilliant colorist Mark Rothko, and Barnett Newman and Ad Reinhardt. These painters rejected the spontaneous approach of the so-called "action painting" technique and meticulously and carefully controlled their effects of color and line. (Examples of the works of all these men are reproduced in color on pages 152-159.)

Whatever their differences in technique, the painters of the New York School endured common frustrations during the '40s and '50s. While they were finding themselves as artists, they continued to suffer neglect by the critics of the art establishment and the ennui and misunderstanding of the public at large. Their work was shown by a considerable number of dealers willing to risk laughter and the critics' barbs, but the prices the dealers were able to obtain were discouragingly low. Peggy Guggenheim recalled some years later that while she had sold a number of Pollocks by 1947 through her Art of This Century gallery, she had never received more than $1,000 for a single one of them. (Two decades later, a large but not particularly important Pollock sold for $150,000.) And while the Modern and a few other museums displayed the New Yorkers' work, popular, traditional institutions like the Metropolitan Museum of Art only rarely showed contemporary paintings.

To overcome this resistance, the artists decided to do a little self-promotion. In 1950 a group of them, quickly labeled "the irascibles," publicly protested the Metropolitan's exhibition policies. Some of them, including Pollock, Motherwell, de Kooning and Rothko, went further, mounting a private show in a rented store in Greenwich Village. The Artists' Club that members of the group had founded in 1949 sponsored discussions and opened a school to bring the message of Abstract Expressionism to younger artists.

None of these efforts proved of much avail. All the self-promoting projects were eventually discontinued, and the artists got back to painting, the business they knew best. In time, however, the art of the New York School came to be accepted for what it was, a successful pursuit of the goal that Pollock had set: "I want to express my feelings rather than illustrate them. Technique is just a means of arriving at a statement." Exactly what statement Pollock was making is a matter for the individual viewer to decide. This is in fact the problem with all truly abstract work; it requires the viewer to participate, to respond without the aid of a recognizable subject or the traditional esthetic values like "finish," or composition. This is, of course, one of the reasons why much of the modern art of the last 20 years has been so difficult to look at and enjoy. The real test of a fully abstract contemporary painting is the amount of meaning and sensation and visual interest it yields as time goes on. Pollock's work, by this measure, stands with the best art of the century.

Pollock himself could not keep up the pace of inventiveness he began with such a fury in 1947. By the early 1950s he had begun to retreat to a kind of figurative abstraction once again involving symbols and myths. He was much disturbed by the problem of advancing his art and, despite increasing acceptance, found it difficult to work in his last few years of life. His drinking problem became severe. In May 1956 Pollock was notified that the Museum of Modern Art would begin a series of one-man shows called "Work in Progress" with an exhibit of up to 25 of his major paintings that fall. Before the show was held Pollock was driving home one night in August after a party when his car veered off a road near his Long Island home. It crashed into a clump of trees and overturned. He was killed instantly.

With Pollock's death his influence did not diminish. Indeed his reputation grew as time passed, inspiring a host of imitators. At the same time, however, many painters began to reject his example, just as Pollock had reacted against Benton and the realists, not to mention the abstractionists who preceded him. Yet whatever their styles, his successors could be grateful to Pollock and his generation for bolstering a self-confident spirit among American artists, establishing a high moral tone for their personal expressions and creating a market for contemporary American abstract painting.

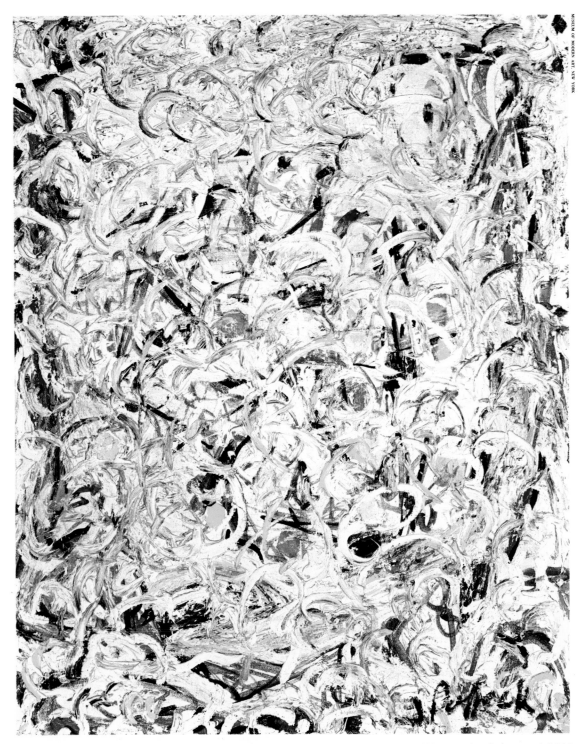

Jackson Pollock: *Sounds in the Grass (Shimmering Substance)*, 1946

# Explosions in Paint

Bound loosely by age, location and a common urge to assert themselves, a group of artists working in New York in the 1940s created the first American style to have worldwide impact on the course of painting. The acknowledged leader of the movement—usually known as Abstract Expressionism—was Jackson Pollock, who made some of the earliest innovations. In bold abstractions like the one above, pulsing with swirls of dashes from edge to edge, he attempted to convey what he called "energy made visible."

Pollock's style, which exploited the whole
surface of the canvas, weaving it together with
skeins of pigment, finally broke the domination
of Renaissance perspective, which had held
back even abstract painting during the earlier
half of the 20th Century. In a Pollock work,
like the one at right, there is no single part to
which the eye is drawn, no one area that is
more important than another; the entire canvas
is the painting. Refusing to allow his hand even
to suggest a regular rhythm or pattern on the
canvas, Pollock overcame the traditional
painter's instinct to create concrete illusions;
instead he sought to contact his deepest feelings
and communicate them in the most vivid and
direct way possible. It was a demanding and
difficult task, but he succeeded, and in so doing
helped to open the way for other artists.

No better description exists of Pollock's
method of working than his own: "My painting
does not come from the easel. . . . I prefer to
tack the unstretched canvas to the wall or floor.
I need the resistance of a hard surface. On the
floor I am more at ease. I feel nearer, more a
part of the painting, since in this way I can
walk around it, work from the four sides and
literally be *in* the painting. This is akin to the
method of the Indian sand painters of the West.

"I continue to get further away from the
usual painter's tools such as easel, palette,
brushes, etc. I prefer sticks, trowels, knives and
dripping fluid paint or a heavy impasto with
sand, broken glass and other foreign matter
added. When I am in my painting, I'm not
aware of what I'm doing. It is only after a sort
of get-acquainted period that I see what I have
been about. I have no fears of making changes,
destroying the image, etc., because the painting
has a life of its own. I try to let it come through.
It is only when I lose contact with the painting
that the result is a mess. Otherwise there is
pure harmony, an easy give and take, and the
painting comes out well."

Jackson Pollock: *Number 6*, 1949

Franz Kline: *Nijinsky*, 1948

Like other "action" painters of the New York School, Franz Kline was extremely individualistic in his choice of a personal style; at the same time, he was sustained by their collective drive to find his own means of expression. In describing the work of some painters whom he admired, Kline said: "The final test of a painting, theirs, mine, any other, is: does the painter's emotion come across?"

Having begun by painting quite traditional landscapes, cityscapes and portraits, Kline in the late 1940s began to refine his style to a vigorous, slashing form of abstraction. In key works like *Nijinsky (near right)*, he showed the beginnings of his transformation: the roughly brushed face and the strong zigzag pattern in the hat (the dancer is dressed in his role as the puppet-clown Petrouchka) show the latent power of the artist's hand. Soon he turned to bold patterns in black and white to convey the powerful emotions that he sought to capture. Like Pollock, Kline found his paintings growing larger and larger. He needed size to express the expansiveness of his imagery and his response to New York City, which he loved, and to the energy of contemporary life; his black-and-white *Requiem (right, center)* is almost nine feet high. Color returned to Kline's work in paintings like *Dahlia (far right)*. In the brilliant and immense *Orange and Black Wall (lower right)* he combined huge size with dazzling color and the powerful black-and-white forms of earlier works, creating, in this case, a bridgelike grid of horizontals and verticals. This late painting, like others of its kind called "wall" paintings, is 12 feet across, almost a wall in itself.

Kline's success was late in coming but, like his work, was large in dimension. Having supported himself as a teacher of art on and off for about 15 years, he began to make sales of paintings to museums in the mid-1950s. In 1960 he was awarded a prize at the Venice Biennale, a mark of considerable international stature. He was not to enjoy his hard-earned fame for long, however: in 1962 he died of a heart condition at the age of 52.

Franz Kline: *Requiem*, 1958

Franz Kline: *Dahlia*, 1959

Franz Kline: *Orange and Black Wall*, 1959

149

Willem de Kooning: *Woman and Bicycle*, 1952-1953

WHITNEY MUSEUM OF AMERICAN ART

Willem de Kooning: *Door to the River*, 1960

Unlike other members of the New York School, Willem de Kooning never totally abandoned recognizable imagery. Figures of women or elements of landscape often appear in his paintings. "Forms," he once said, "ought to have the emotion of concrete experience." His work is not representational, however, for he is totally uninterested in creating simply the illusion of flesh or fields. For him, forms emerge as he paints; he once declared, for example, that the women in his works had large breasts solely because his arm moved naturally in large curves. While his painting at the left has traces of savage humor, it is as much about texture, light and color as about women. Similarly, in paintings like *Door to the River (above)*, the title seems to suggest a specific image but the subject is by no means a river.

151

Clyfford Still: *1947J*

Clyfford Still abandoned representational painting early in the 1940s and began to evolve a highly distinctive style characterized by jagged, flamelike shapes and heavily textured backgrounds laid on with a knife instead of a brush. He also abandoned titles for his works, preferring to label them simply with the year and an alphabetical designation. Thus, the work above was the 10th he completed in 1947. Clearly the statement of a determined, moody personality, Still's work conveys a sense of the individual's assertion of himself in a hostile world.

Philip Guston's painting reflects what one observer

Philip Guston: *The Mirror*, 1957

calls "a dialogue between subject and abstract structure." But the "subject" is never merely a tree, a figure or, as the title of the painting above indicates, a mirror. It can be a form, a shape or a color, for although Guston sometimes begins depicting realistic objects, he does not complete them. His real subject is painting and himself. "The pressing thing for me in painting is 'When are you through?'" Guston says. "I would like to think a picture is finished when it feels not new, but old. As if its forms had lived a long time in you, even though until it appears you did not know what it would look like."

153

Adolph Gottlieb: *Blast I*, 1957

Robert Motherwell: *Elegy to the Spanish Republic, No. 102*, 1965

Defining the dilemma of the contemporary painter, Robert Motherwell once said, "We modern artists have no generally accepted subject matter, no inherited iconography. But to re-invent painting, its subject matter and its means, is a task so difficult that one must reduce it to a very simple concept in order to paint for the sheer joy of painting, as simple as the Madonna was to many generations of painters."

Following this credo, Motherwell and another New York painter, Adolph Gottlieb, present their work mostly in the form of large, clearly defined shapes of varying size and color. Motherwell, who also works in collage, deals in extremely flat shapes, usually on a solid ground. In the work above, one of a long series he did called "Elegy to the Spanish Republic," he created strong tension by squeezing lozengelike forms between irregular verticals that bend and resist the swelling pressure. At the left, Gottlieb placed an evanescent round shape above a chaos of rough, interwoven strokes; the result suggests both a sun rising over a city and an atomic explosion bursting above devastation.

In their use of such bold, simple forms, Gottlieb and Motherwell stand opposed to painters like Pollock, Kline and de Kooning. No less expressive, this is their way out of the dilemma.

Mark Rothko: *#18*, 1949

Mark Rothko, a Russian-born painter who died in New York in 1970, once observed that "there are some painters who want to tell all, but I feel it is more shrewd to tell little. My paintings are sometimes described as façades, and, indeed, they are façades."

In arriving at his mature style, Rothko developed a soft and sensuous approach to color, usually applied in diaphanous washes and organized roughly in three fuzzy-edged rectangles, as in the work above at right. Earlier, he had adopted a less formal imagery *(left)*.

Mark Rothko: *Yellow and Gold,* 1956

Well before the flowering of Abstract Expressionism, he and Adolph Gottlieb made a summing-up statement: "We favor the simple expression of the complex thought. We are for the large shape because it has the impact of the unequivocal. We wish to reassert the picture plane. We are for flat forms because they destroy illusion and reveal truth." Rothko added: "I paint large pictures because I want to create . . . intimacy. A large picture is an immediate transaction; it takes you into it."

Ad Reinhardt: *Black Painting*, 1960-1966

At the opposite pole from painters of broad gestures and violent colors are Ad Reinhardt and Barnett Newman, both of whom adopted an austere attitude. Reinhardt, in the five-foot canvas shown above, painted nine squares of subtly different dark colors. In his *Twelve Rules for a New Academy*, written in the late 1950s, he advised artists to reject all the traditional tools: texture, brushwork, drawing, forms, design, color, light, space, time, scale, movement, subject. His art, which seems nothing less than anti-art, is in fact the expression of a dedicated purist. Interested in the interaction of colors, Newman reduces his works to flat fields relieved only by a few contrasting stripes *(opposite)*.

Barnett Newman: *Who's Afraid of Red, Yellow, Blue I*, 1966

# VII

# The Soup Can School

In the spring of 1961 a few enterprising art dealers in New York City began to promote a style that was as different from Abstract Expressionism, the reigning movement, as a rock 'n' roll song was from an intricately structured concerto. The new art broke sharply from pure abstraction by returning to recognizable subject matter, as earlier American realists had done. But what subject matter! Soup cans and Coke bottles, street signs and light bulbs, comic-strip characters and movie stars—all were represented in exaggerated detail, blown up sometimes to heroic size on canvases that seemed to glory in the banalities of American life. In some cases, objects were even tacked on as appendages to the paintings for added three-dimensional impact. To many observers the whole freewheeling madness looked like a put-on, if not some kind of sinister plot. In fact, what public criticism the young, unknown practitioners of this art managed to draw came mainly in the form of derisive sniffs and snorts. Their exhibitions were few and their sales even fewer.

The new style, however, was not to be denied. By the spring of 1963 the newly established Gallery of Modern Art in Washington, D.C., had organized a show displaying the works of a dozen of the New York artists, who by then were marching under the banner of "Pop," so named for the popular, or common, objects they used in their works. Pop was as yet far from popular in the public sense; indeed, it still befuddled most observers, as the Washington exhibit soon proved. Incongruously set in a rambling Victorian mansion, the show featured such works as a King Kong-sized pair of trousers made out of canvas and bright-blue acrylic paint and a painting with a real armchair attached to it. The opening-night crowd gulped its complimentary champagne in silence. Then a few of the guests cautiously began to take turns sitting in the armchair. A small boy turned on a working television set that was bolted to another canvas and watched a baseball game. At one point during the evening, a guest almost got in a fistfight with the artist Jim Dine after the man had emptied his champagne glass into a sink that Dine had hooked up to one of his paintings. Reviewing the proceedings the next day in the *Washington Star*, critic Frank Getlein wrote: "Pop's a flop." At that point critical reaction to the movement as a whole was hardly better. Surrealist painter Max Ernst sighed: "Pop art is just some feeble bubbles of flat Coca-Cola which I consider less than interesting and rather sad." Henry Seldis of *The Los Angeles Times* wrote that Pop "is painting of a sort; it may even be art, but it is certainly poor art." TIME, calling the movement a "cult of the commonplace," observed haughtily that "Pop art has exposed as rarely before the wholesale gullibility of the kind of people who fear that unless they embrace every passing novelty they will some day be labeled Philistine."

Implicit in this frosty critical reception, of course, was the feeling that the mass-produced objects and images of an industrial culture were simply unworthy of serious artistic attention. The Pop artists did not agree. They had grown up in a world of Coke bottles and comic books; these, they felt, were the uniquely American images of their times. And gradually, they began to succeed in getting the point across. But when James Rosenquist sold an oversized Pop mural for $1,400, he was so surprised at receiving that much money that he joked about not having to pay a storage fee for the work.

By the spring of 1965 Pop had grown to such a degree that it had muscled Abstract Expressionism out of many major galleries. Some Pop artists, notably Andy Warhol, Roy Lichtenstein and Claes Oldenburg, in a couple of years had achieved more publicity—if not widespread admiration—than most leading Abstract Expressionists had received in a decade. The public, whether it actually understood Pop or not, seemed willing to have a little fun with it, and was soon swept up in a host of fads built around the movement's trappings. Passengers on Braniff Airlines flew in jetliners whose exteriors were painted in the bright pastel shades favored by Pop artists. Taking a hint from Lichtenstein's cartoonlike panels *(page 160)*, some young entrepreneurs blew up drawings of the comic-book heroes Flash Gordon, the Phantom, Mandrake the Magician and Prince Valiant and, offering them as posters, sold 4,000 in three weeks. Although some reviewers still scoffed, many critics began to treat the movement with a wary respect. John Canaday perceptively observed in *The New York Times:* "Pop was rooted in a revival and translation of legitimate values. . . . As a deadpan comment on the comic strips, the canning industry, the girlie calendar, the signboard and the TV commercial, Pop has been alternately entertaining and offensive. But it has been important as a return to pictorial subject matter shifted into contemporary focus. . . . Pop as a reference to a visual world familiar to all of us has struck its roots firmly."

That same spring, Rosenquist achieved the ultimate in commercial respectability: he sold an 85-foot mural entitled *F-111* for $60,000. There are no reports that he made jokes this time.

Tracing Pop art's growth in comparison to that of other movements is like watching a time-lapse nature film in which a flower blossoms in seconds—no movement in art history ever developed from birth to middle age with such incredible speed. The forces that led to its creation are relatively easy to pinpoint. The reasons for its subsequent acceptance, first by dealers and collectors and then by the public, are considerably more complex.

In the mid-1950s many younger painters were growing disillusioned with Abstract Expressionism; they were frustrated by the limitations of a movement that had dominated American art for more than a decade. The critic Clement Greenberg analyzed the reasons: "What turned this constellation of stylistic features into something bad as art was its standardization, its reduction to a set of mannerisms, as a dozen, and then a thousand, artists proceeded to maul the same viscosities of paint, in more or less the same ranges of color, and with the same 'gestures,' into the same kind of picture."

About that time Jasper Johns and Robert Rauschenberg, two artists who had studios in the same New York loft building, began to introduce mundane objects into their work, either painting them quite realistically or actually attaching them to their paintings. Although retaining the Abstract Expressionists' characteristic concern for surface textures, Johns began to depict objects like flags, targets and numbers *(page 170)*. At the same time, Rauschenberg started to construct "combines," in which he integrated real three-dimensional objects like street signs with his painted canvases *(page 169)*. The works of these two men during this period were not so much Pop as precursors of it, signals that a major break was at hand.

By the late 1950s other New York artists had begun to experiment on their own. They shared certain things in common—backgrounds in commercial art that ranged from fashion illustrator (Warhol) to billboard painter (Rosenquist), a knowledge of what Johns and Rauschenberg were doing, and a fascination with the images of popular culture. They were influenced not only by such standard sources of advertisements as television and magazines, but also by the city street scene—particularly the huge animated displays and neon signs of Times Square, including a 22-foot-high face that puffed smoke rings for Camel cigarettes and a 140-foot-long rooftop waterfall that refreshed for Pepsi-Cola. In their work these artists transferred intact many of the images, techniques, colors and scale of advertising art. Andy Warhol meticulously re-created on canvas one of Pop's most memorable symbols, a can of Campbell's soup as it might appear in a magazine ad—but he lifted it out of magazine context and made it an unsettling three feet high. Rosenquist incorporated into his gargantuan murals such garish images as orange mounds of spaghetti, pouty lips smeared with scarlet lipstick, and incredibly long and perfect legs right out of a nylon stocking ad. Claes Oldenburg went to king-sized "soft" sculpture as his specialty, stuffing canvas with kapok to create huge, wildly colored replicas of hamburgers, popsicles, chocolate cream pies and other all-American staples.

Such eye-catching concoctions soon caught the attention of a handful of modern-art dealers on the lookout for something new. Throughout the 1950s art galleries had proliferated in New York, and with the founding of each new one the search for new ideas and new artists intensified. Two of the more adventurous searchers in the city were Leo Castelli, owner of the Castelli Gallery, and Richard Bellamy, who was shortly to open the Green Gallery. Castelli was an entrepreneur of considerable talent; his friend Willem de Kooning, the Abstract Expressionist, reportedly once said of him: "He has the nerve to sell anything. He could even sell beer cans." (After hearing of de Kooning's facetious crack, Jasper Johns proceeded to make a sculpture of two Ballantine Ale cans in painted bronze, and Castelli managed to sell it for a price in the four-figure range.) Toward the end of the decade, during their treks from one artist's loft to another, the two men noticed the emerging trend; soon afterward, each began to promote it. Their judgments proved shrewd.

The art market at that time was a one-way escalator moving steadily upward. Business in general was good, and art, as is often the case in good times, was a much sought-after commodity for investment. The masters of Abstract Expressionism were commanding extravagant prices—major Jackson Pollock paintings were selling for more than $100,000—and even minor works were fetching $5,000 to $10,000. Castelli and Bellamy soon found a few customers who were willing to experiment, especially at prices substantially lower than those commanded by the Abstract Expressionists. Among Pop art's earliest purchasers were such established collectors as Philip Johnson, the architect; Harry Abrams, a publisher of high-quality art books; Burton Tremaine, an industrialist; and attorney Leon Mnuchin. One of the most publicized collectors, however, was Leon Kraushar, an insurance executive who crammed his Long Island home with some 200 Pop paintings and sculptures, then publicly compared his rapidly appreciating collection to IBM stock; another was Robert Scull, a taxicab magnate whose entrance into jet-set society roughly coincided with his first major Pop purchases.

Although the motives of these men may have varied, each seemed to regard his collection with genuine enjoyment. "What Pop art has done for me is to make the world a pleasanter place to live in," Johnson enthusiastically proclaimed. "I look at things with an entirely different eye—at Coney Island, at billboards, at Coca-Cola bottles. One of the duties of art is to make you look at the world with pleasure. Pop art is the only movement in this century that has tried to do it." Abrams discussed the movement in more philosophical terms: "A good Pop painting will always remain a work of art, and it has nothing to do with whether it's identified with a certain era or a commercial subject. Too many people attach importance to the subject of a painting instead of to the art. The difference between what's beautiful and what's ugly depends on the context of our looking at it. Someone who's never seen either a wine bottle or a Coca-Cola bottle would find them equally beautiful. But Cézanne's wine bottle holds a higher key than Warhol's Coke bottle because we associate one with gracious living and we've seen the other in supermarkets."

Once it had the support of dealers and collectors, Pop art took off.

Its success was perhaps due as much to the craze for something new —and to the efficiency of the mass media, which found it made good, light copy—as to the inherent qualities of the art itself. But there was no question that the works produced by the movement plucked responsive chords at the particular time they appeared.

In the first place, the visual acuity of Americans had been gradually expanded by television, and Pop above all else relied on instant, highly visual impressions. In addition to beaming fact and fiction into living rooms all over America, TV had been heightening people's sensitivity to images; with its abrupt juxtapositions, it was conducting a sort of speed-reading course in pictures rather than words. The lesson was rapid scanning and retention, and the test, which the public took night after night, was coping with the barrage of separate images, which within a two-minute stretch of commercials might run as high as 50. With this kind of conditioning, it is not surprising that viewers took to Pop; in contrast with Abstract Expressionism, often a highly intellectual exercise, Pop was easy to grasp at a glance.

At the same time, the whole attitude of Pop, from its shiny colors to its whimsical humor, had ample parallels in the nation's changing life style. In the 1960s, kitchen appliances were being sold not only in time-honored white but in a rainbow of other colors as well; automobiles streamed off Detroit assembly lines in brighter and brighter hues. The Beatles were setting off an explosion not only in music but in a flippant, engaging and essentially playful approach toward a too-serious world. A fad for trivia was built on remembering useless scraps of nostalgia (e.g., the fact that in the old "Lone Ranger" programs, "Scout" was the name of Tonto's horse; that the name of Batman's butler was "Alfred"). "Camp," a closely related phenomenon, revived interest in everything from the fashions of the 1930s to watching reruns of old Tarzan movies on television. Pop was readily embraced in the atmosphere of the times.

Much of the good-natured acceptance of Pop was engineered by the artists themselves. Few artists in history have so consciously touted themselves and their works; compared with the introverted Abstract Expressionists, Pop painters were like bikinied starlets on the prowl for photographers at a film festival. Epitomizing the artist as self-promoter were Andy Warhol and Claes Oldenburg. Warhol cultivated his reputation for being enigmatic by hiding behind oversized sunglasses and by churning out eight-hour films on such stationary subjects as a sleeping man and the Empire State Building between dusk and midnight. Oldenburg staged a series of "Happenings," Dadaist-inspired gatherings at which seemingly random sights and sounds—verses of a song, clips from a movie, a poetry reading, parts of a ballet—were made to "happen" in an apparently unrelated sequence. The major reason that this self-publicity succeeded was that it had a deft tongue-in-cheek character, a fashionable hip quality.

On occasion, the public's reasons for accepting Pop were not precisely what the artists intended. The Pop painter Tom Wesselmann once complained that "some of the worst things said about Pop Art

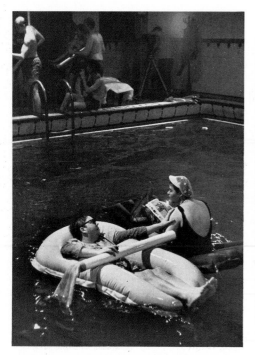

Pop artist Claes Oldenburg was one of the first practitioners of an art form called "Happenings," zany mixtures of theater, dance, kinetic sculpture and vaudeville. In the photograph above, Metropolitan Museum curator Henry Geldzahler floats with a friend in the pool of a New York health club during one Oldenburg production. At right above is a scene from "Stars," an event that Oldenburg staged at the Washington, D.C., Gallery of Modern Art in 1963; an awkward waiter carries a huge tray of food that he is about to spill over the unsuspecting audience (the "food," fortunately, proved to be bits of chopped plastic).

have come from its admirers; they begin to sound like some nostalgia cult—they really worship Marilyn Monroe or Coca-Cola." In fact, the public dwelt on the nostalgic images because Pop paintings seldom involved viewers in their content—a circumstance for which the artists were, through their techniques, deliberately responsible.

The movement's most visible trademark was its bedrock simplicity. That is not to say that Pop works were necessarily shallow or unsubtle, but the Pop artists stressed instant graspability in their compositions. The extraneous, distracting elements that they purged from their paintings even included their signatures, which are found on the backs of most of their works.

In addition, Pop had a highly detached air. The basic materials used by the movement's artists—enamel and acrylic paints, plastics and vinyls—imparted to their works a glossy smoothness closely related to the cold, two-dimensional images perceived on a television screen or on the pages of a magazine. Pop artists intensified this slickness by moving ever further away from traditional concerns with paint and canvas textures. Most labored to smooth away any traces of brushstrokes. Some, like Warhol, tried to achieve complete impersonality by turning to such mechanical processes as silk-screening, in which an image is transferred to a silk-screen stencil and then varicolored inks are forced through the screen onto canvas or paper.

Finally, Pop works seemed as anonymous as the committee-created advertisements and objects they memorialized. Spontaneity was an asset to the artists only while they conceived a painting; once they began to execute their conceptions, they rigidly observed the style of the original. To make sure of this, many Pop painters used draftsmanlike techniques. Some employed projectors to blow up their sketches, then meticulously traced the enlarged original. Others borrowed the billboard painters' method of gridding, in which the preliminary sketch and the final surface are marked off in identically shaped rectangles,

and the design transferred, grid by grid. Commercial techniques so permeated all phases of Pop art that Roy Lichtenstein simulated one of them, Benday dots, in his paintings. In actual commercial printing, tiny dots of primary colors are spaced closely together; when they are viewed from a distance, they merge to form additional colors and shadings. Lichtenstein, using specially prepared metal stencils that were perforated with holes, painted regularly spaced dots of considerable size on his canvases.

Despite the emphasis on technique, however, the execution of a Pop work was not as important as its inspiration, its theme. This premium on original conception meant, for example, that once Warhol had done soup cans, they became his property and no one else's; and, in a sense, any painting depicting a brand-name product suspended in mid-canvas and painted in a flat, unadorned style was "a Warhol," and of negligible value unless signed by him. By the same token, any cartoonlike painting properly belonged to Lichtenstein. This highly personal vision based largely on subject matter was the real signature of each major Pop artist; Pop was generally united as a movement more by themes than by styles.

But because in Pop art the subject matter was so common and personal painting style so de-emphasized, many artists of meager talent tried to cash in. Few succeeded. In their clumsy attempts, though, which ranged from paintings to posters to clothes and even to dishes and cups, they began to bludgeon to death a movement that depended on uniqueness and a light touch.

By the mid-1960s Pop had already been so worked over that two new movements, Op and Minimal art, had appeared to challenge it. Both were reactions to Pop, in that they swung back again to abstraction; yet both were also continuations of Pop, in that they emphasized a detached anonymity, employed the colors of commercial paints, and featured hard edges and surface brightness.

Enthusiastic Pop collectors Leon Kraushar and Robert Scull found their purchases easy to live with. In the picture at left, Kraushar *(reclining on sofa)* and his wife entertain art dealer Ben Birillo in a living room crammed with such works as John Chamberlain's junked auto, George Segal's life-sized plaster figures, Andy Warhol's Brillo boxes and sculptures by Roy Lichtenstein and Claes Oldenburg. Above, Scull and his wife, standing before a Jasper Johns flag painting, inspect a dinner that can never be served: the food, catered by Oldenburg, is all painted plaster.

Op, or Optical, art was a catchall for a wide variety of styles based on scientific principles of color and pattern perception. One branch of the movement seemed to be a deliberate assault on the viewer's retina, an attempt to create, through juxtapositions of intense colors and/or geometric designs, afterimages or a sense of pulsating movement. Unintentional examples of this style appear in many encyclopedias and textbooks. In one common illustration, a green heart with a yellow border appears on a gray background. If the reader stares at this image for a period of time and then looks at a white wall, he will see an afterimage of a red heart with a blue border, the complementary colors of the original.

As some Op paintings were intense, even irritating, so Minimal works were reserved in their striving to call attention to the subtleties of colors. Some artists interwove gay, bright hues into playful geometric designs; others painted in pale tones that stressed slight gradations in one color; still others created monochromatic canvases that recalled the "black" paintings of Ad Reinhardt *(page 158)*. To many viewers, Op and Minimal works were initially intriguing, but lacked interest on second or third viewings; in any event, the movements never attained the high spirits and popularity of Pop.

By the beginning of the 1970s, still other movements had emerged to capture the attention of the American art public. Some of them were inspired by museums searching as never before for catchy exhibition themes; some were initiated by art dealers anxious for new merchandise. By far the most numerous and convincing expressions, however, came from the artists themselves as they explored uncharted territory. Conceptual, Environmental, Photo-Realism, Kinetic—all these terms were applied in the art magazines and news journals to what was happening. The same debate raged over each new expression: Was it, or wasn't it, Art?

The problem was that in the midst of all the energetic innovation, American artists again stood in the perplexing position of having almost too many possibilities open to them. With Abstract Expressionism had come the artist's freedom to put anything he wanted on canvas —or in metal or neon or plastic, for that matter—and call it art. With that freedom had come a concomitant obligation—to find his own means and mode of expression. But with the new freedom also came a new attitude of acceptance among the public, a relaxed, "wait-and-see" philosophy that allowed the artist to make his statement without immediately having to stand up to the criteria of the ages.

In such an atmosphere art buffs and collectors could find delight in the varied and inventive expressions of fresh talent as well as in the continued achievements of veteran artists painting in already accepted styles. As of 1970 no one could determine the probable future course of art, even over the short term. But with a broadening and increasingly sophisticated audience, with better training and facilities for artists, and with improving scholarly and critical machinery to evaluate, document and catalogue new work, the future of American art seemed full of promise.

Robert Rauschenberg: *Black Market,* 1961

# From Pop to Op

Robert Rauschenberg bridged Abstract Expressionism and the newer Pop movement. Rauschenberg broke from abstraction by fastening to his canvases such real, and mundane, objects as rusting signs and license plates *(above)*. The effect of this arrangement of objects, called a "combine," led many viewers to experience, as the London *Observer* put it, "a feeling of some subliminal message being flashed from the canvas, something too quick for anything but the imagination to record."

Jasper Johns: *Numbers in Color*, 1958-1959

The early works of Jasper Johns were as responsible for the shift from pure abstraction as Rauschenberg's "combines." Unlike the combines, however, Johns's paintings are traditionally two-dimensional. He chose subjects that seldom received the artist's attention—flags, targets, maps, numbers *(left)*. "I was concerned," he said, "with the invisibility those images had acquired, and the idea of knowing an image rather than just seeing it out of the corner of your eye."

In later works Johns also adopted the "combine" idea and showed his fascination with his craft by making painting itself a subject. The witty *Field Painting (right)* proffers its own history. Red, yellow and blue—the primaries from which the welter of other colors are derived—are spelled out both as three-dimensional cutouts and as words stenciled on the canvas. Attached to the raised letters are the tools used in the painting. Johns integrated stage directions into the work to ensure proper hanging, and even built in a light source: the raised letter "R" is a neon light controlled by the imbedded light switch. Finally, the artist added bits of his own biography to that of his painting; the ale can and the coffee tin refer to well-known Johns sculptures.

Jasper Johns: *Field Painting*, 1963-1964

Robert Indiana: *American Gas Works*, 1961-1962

The terse, ubiquitous signs that inform or command us in our daily lives have strongly influenced Robert Indiana and Allan D'Arcangelo, two artists whose work is often classified as Pop. Indiana is best known for posterlike canvases; the one above was inspired

by a stencil that a New York utility company used in the 19th Century to identify its property; the numbered circles copy the dials on a gas meter.

D'Arcangelo's special preserve is the American road. His early paintings are haunting evocations of

Allan D'Arcangelo: *Proposition No. 9*, 1966

the highway at dusk, deserted ribbons of pavement flowing endlessly toward clefts carved out of the horizon. In a later phase, he focused on the signs that march wordlessly beside the road. *Proposition No. 9 (above)*, one of a series of clean, spare abstractions, shows D'Arcangelo's fascination with perspective. The tapering black shapes that form a base to the composition suggest a highway disappearing into infinity; the S-curve sign, split in half, seems to jump through the driver's windshield.

COLLECTION HARRY N. ABRAMS, NEW YORK

Larry Rivers: *Dutch Masters and Cigars II*, 1963

Painters as different in style as Larry Rivers and Andy Warhol found common ground on at least one occasion in their interest in American package designs. *Dutch Masters and Cigars II (left)* is Rivers' interpretation of Rembrandt's classic portrait of a group of Dutch burghers as they appear on boxes of Dutch Masters' cigars. The artist filled his eight-foot-tall canvas with fragmented, ghostly images. Rivers works hard to achieve this smudgy quality; he once said, "I have had a bad arm and am not interested in the art of holding up mirrors."

Best known of the Pop artists, Andy Warhol has likened himself to a machine; he deliberately strives to obliterate the painter's touch from his works. The painting below is one of his more relaxed efforts; instead of presenting a single large can of Campbell's Soup head on—the Pop symbol for which he became famous—he has stacked four cans, of different varieties, in seemingly haphazard fashion—and even opened one of them.

Andy Warhol: *Four Campbell's Soup Cans*, 1962

ooking at a James Rosenquist mural is like looking at an old billboard on which sections of a new advertisement are being painted: both contain recognizable but bizarrely juxtaposed images. In the late 1950s, Rosenquist actually worked as a billboard painter, executing such assignments as a 20-by-58-foot portrait of the actress Joanne Woodward as an advertisement for one of her movies. Later, in his own works, he deliberately retained many of the billboard artist's techniques. His paintings are king-sized, done with garish colors in flat areas, and his images mimic advertising styles. The 7-by-11-foot *Nomad (right)* typifies what Rosenquist tries to cram into his works: "The flicker of chrome. Reflectives. Quick flashes of light. The first visual response. Quick decisions. Rapid associations." *Nomad* blends, from left to right, part of a detergent box, two pairs of ballerinas' legs, a redwood picnic table and bench, a huge billfold, a mass of spaghetti with meatballs and olives, part of a light bulb, a microphone, and the stake of some unseen sign rising from a patch of grass. The artist has also tacked on a plastic refuse bag *(upper left)* and a pile of sticks he used to mix paints for the mural *(lower left)*. Though, taken singly, the images seem clear enough, Rosenquist has placed them so that they become a cascade of impressions.

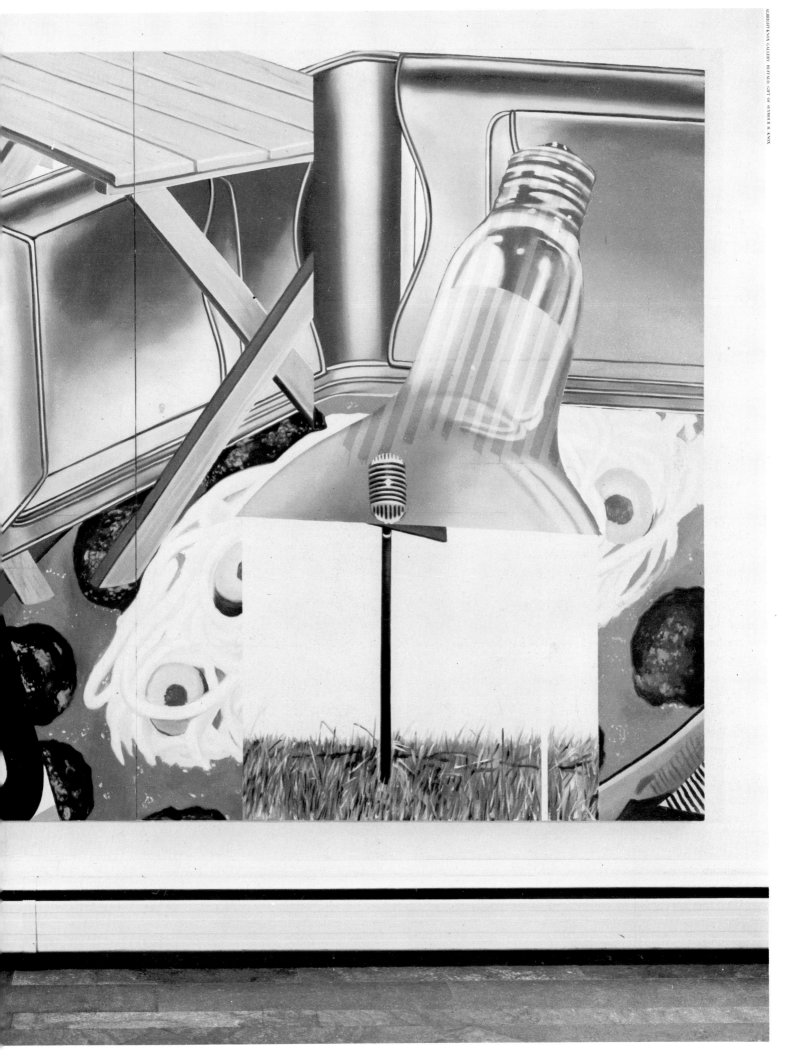

James Rosenquist: *Nomad*, 1963

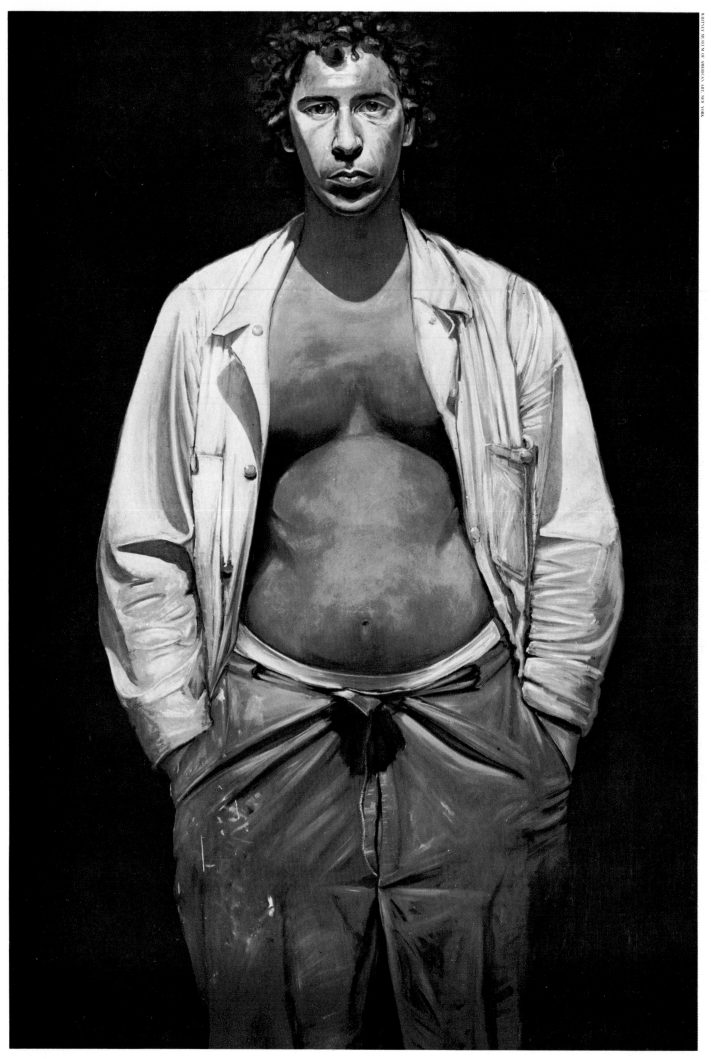

Alfred Leslie: *Alfred Leslie*, 1966-1967

Howard Kanovitz: *The Dance*, 1965

**P**ainting that seems to be photographic has been called Super-Realism, or, as one critic has named it, Leica-ism. *Alfred Leslie (left)*, a self-portrait, is marked by a starkness typical of that artist's work. But Leslie, who paints harshly lighted figures on canvases as large as six by nine feet, achieves subtle distortions: he views head, chest, abdomen and thighs from eye level and paints each separately.

For his effects, Howard Kanovitz composes group paintings by making studies from actual photographs. But *The Dance (above)*, partly inspired by the celebration of a nephew's *bar mitzvah*, includes surprising portraits of former Supreme Court Justice Abe Fortas *(upper left)* and the writer Fannie Hurst *(upper right)*. Kanovitz has portrayed himself in the foreground, dancing with his wife.

Three traditional genres—figure painting, the nude and the self-portrait—were reworked in the 1960s in highly idiosyncratic ways by Richard Lindner, Tom Wesselmann and Jim Dine.

Lindner specializes in bizarre women. As the critic Grace Glueck points out, "The women he paints are not exactly those a nice boy would bring home to Mummy." In both *Untitled II* and *Coney Island II (below)*, perverse tribute is paid to a pair of belted, helmeted, leather-encased furies whom no one would bring home to Mummy or anyone else. Lindner professes no hatred of females; rather, he says, "I feel sorry for women. When I dress women in these corsets and contraptions in my painting, it's kind of the way I see them wrapping themselves up."

Tom Wesselmann has quite another view of the human female; in his paintings, wanton pink ladies, faceless except for garishly lipsticked mouths, cavort among odd assortments of commercial products *(top, right)*. By blending one of his laughing girls with brightly colored nightstand paraphernalia in *Great American Nude No. 98* Wesselmann suggests a kind of Pop vision of woman as a sex machine.

Dine's subject matter, on the other hand, is almost always himself. His "self-portrait" at bottom right, scarcely a conventional one, is more like a brightly colored advertisement for men's bathrobes. The two chains hung from the necks are objects Dine happened to find. He repeated his bathrobe motif in a series of self-portraits because, he once explained engagingly, "It's a remembered symbol that is important because it keeps coming back."

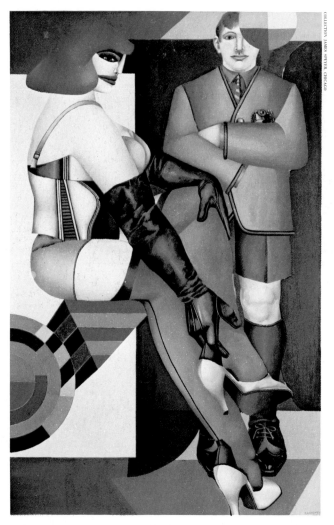

Richard Lindner: *Untitled II*, 1962

Richard Lindner: *Coney Island II*, 1964

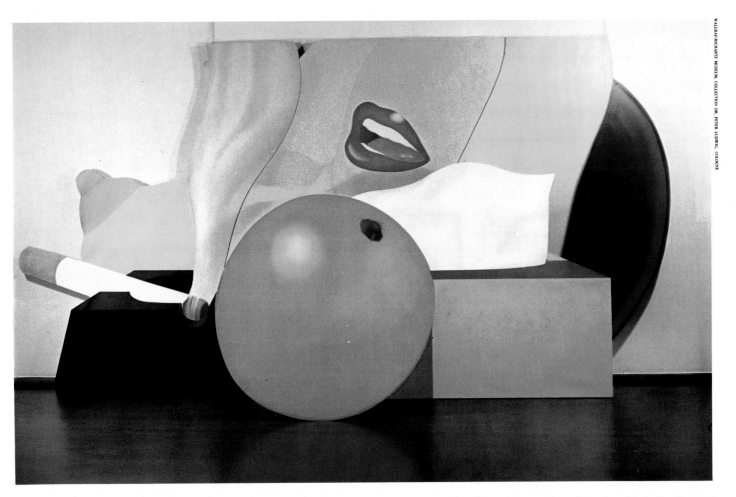

Tom Wesselmann: *Great American Nude No. 98*, 1967

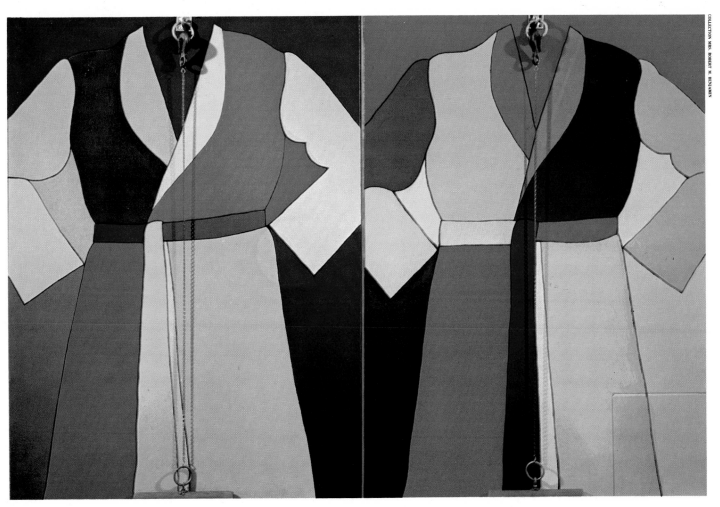

Jim Dine: *Double Isometric Self-Portrait (Serape)*, 1965

The austere mechanical styles that succeeded Pop in the public eye, Op and Minimal art, emerged in the mid-1960s, and hinged, in the words of Josef Albers, on "making colors do something they don't do themselves." Albers, an influential teacher of young artists, had begun to experiment with color interactions in the 1920s. His *Homage to the Square: "Ascending" (below)* is one of a long series of paintings whose formal structure is reduced to squares within squares but whose variety of subtle tonal

illusions is vast. Here, for example, the bottom and side bands of the gray and the blue rectangles appear darker than the upper bands. Actually the colors are uniform throughout.

While Op and Minimal artists are all primarily colorists, their resemblances cease there. Richard Anuszkiewicz, who studied with Albers, relies upon geometric patterns to produce illusory effects. In his *Union of the Four (opposite, upper left)*, four purple squares seem to hover above a red field. The artist

Josef Albers: *Homage to the Square: "Ascending,"* 1953

achieved this not by changing the red, which is constant, but by altering the color of the intersecting lines. Among the purchasers of Anuszkiewicz's eye-teasing works is at least one ophthalmologist.

To create his illusions, Leon Polk Smith places strong colors side by side, producing a sense of pulsation *(upper right)*. To Kenneth Noland, another onetime student of Albers, "the thing in painting is to find a way to get color down, to float it without bogging the painting down in . . . systems of structure"; in *Provence (bottom left)* he achieves a feeling of openness, of colors expanding outward. Al Held has been called a "geometric expressionist"; his works, like the one at bottom right, are large-scale canvases dominated by clean, bright areas of color that almost overshadow fragments of other hues that peep out from unexpected places. In his painting reproduced on the following page, Frank Stella enhances the intensity of each hue by carefully worked juxtapositions of fluorescent colors.

Richard Anuszkiewicz: *Union of the Four*, 1963

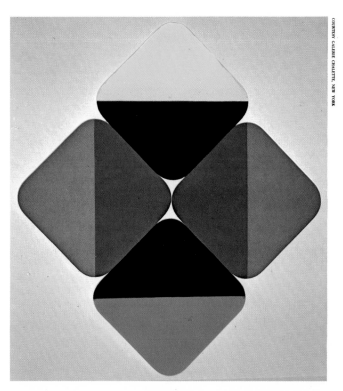

Leon Polk Smith: *Constellation*, 1969

Kenneth Noland: *Provence*, 1960

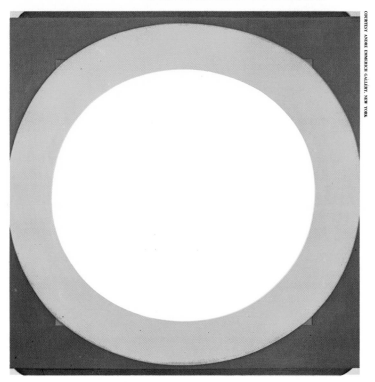

Al Held: *Mao*, 1967

Frank Stella: *Sinjerli Variation II*, 1968

# Chronology: Artists of the 20th Century

| 1865 | 1900 | 1935 | 1970 | 1865 | 1900 | 1935 | 1970 |

**UNITED STATES**

MAURICE PRENDERGAST  1859-1924
ARTHUR B. DAVIES  1862-1928
ROBERT HENRI  1865-1929
GEORGE B. LUKS  1867-1933
ALFRED MAURER  1868-1932
WILLIAM GLACKENS  1870-1938
JOHN MARIN  1870-1953
JOHN SLOAN  1871-1951
LYONEL FEININGER  1871-1956
ERNEST LAWSON  1873-1939
EVERETT SHINN  1876-1953
MARSDEN HARTLEY  1877-1943
JOSEPH STELLA  1877-1946
ARTHUR B. DOVE  1880-1946
HANS HOFMANN  1880-1966
MORTON SCHAMBERG  1881-1918
MAX WEBER  1881-1961
GEORGE BELLOWS  1882-1925
ARTHUR B. CARLES  1882-1952
EDWARD HOPPER  1882-1967
CHARLES DEMUTH  1883-1935
CHARLES SHEELER  1883-1965
GEORGIA O'KEEFFE  1887-
JOSEF ALBERS  1888-1976
THOMAS HART BENTON  1889-1975
STANTON MACDONALD-WRIGHT  1890-1973
MAN RAY  1890-1976
MARK TOBEY  1890-1976
GRANT WOOD  1892-1942
MILTON AVERY  1893-1965
CHARLES BURCHFIELD  1893-1967
STUART DAVIS  1894-1964
JOHN STEUART CURRY  1897-1946
REGINALD MARSH  1898-1954
BEN SHAHN  1898-1969
BRADLEY WALKER TOMLIN  1899-1953
FRITZ GLARNER  1899-1972
RAPHAEL SOYER  1899-
PHILIP EVERGOOD  1901-1973
MARK ROTHKO  1903-1970
ADOLPH GOTTLIEB  1903-1974
ARSHILE GORKY  1904-1948
WILLEM DE KOONING  1904-
CLYFFORD STILL  1904-
BARNETT NEWMAN  1905-1970

**UNITED STATES** (continued)

BURGOYNE DILLER  1906-1965
PETER BLUME  1906-
FRANZ KLINE  1910-1962
MORRIS GRAVES  1910-
JACKSON POLLOCK  1912-1956
AD REINHARDT  1913-1967
HYMAN BLOOM  1913-
PHILIP GUSTON  1913-
JACK LEVINE  1915-
ROBERT MOTHERWELL  1915-
RICHARD POUSETTE-DART  1916-
JACOB LAWRENCE  1917-
ANDREW WYETH  1917-
GEORGE TOOKER  1920-
SAM FRANCIS  1923-
ROY LICHTENSTEIN  1923-
KENNETH NOLAND  1924-
ROBERT RAUSCHENBERG  1925-
HELEN FRANKENTHALER  1928-
ROBERT INDIANA  1928-
RICHARD ANUSZKIEWICZ  1930-
JASPER JOHNS  1930-
ANDY WARHOL  c. 1930-
TOM WESSELMAN  1931-
JAMES ROSENQUIST  1933-
JIM DINE  1935-
FRANK STELLA  1936-

**SPAIN**

PABLO PICASSO  1881-1973
JUAN GRIS  1887-1927
JOAN MIRÓ  1893-
SALVADOR DALI  1904-

**SWITZERLAND**

PAUL KLEE  1879-1940
ALBERTO GIACOMETTI  1901-1966

**GERMANY**

LOVIS CORINTH  1858-1925
EMIL NOLDE  1867-1956
ERNST LUDWIG KIRCHNER  1880-1938
MAX BECKMANN  1884-1950
MAX ERNST  1891-1976
HANS HARTUNG  1904-
WOLS (WOLFGANG SCHULZE)  1913-1951

**HOLLAND**

PIET MONDRIAN  1872-1944

| 1865 | 1900 | 1935 | 1970 | 1865 | 1900 | 1935 | 1970 |

*American artists of the 20th Century and their contemporaries are grouped chronologically according to country. The bands correspond to the life spans of the artists.*

**BELGIUM**
JAMES ENSOR 1860-1949
PAUL DELVAUX 1897-
RENÉ MAGRITTE 1898-1967

**ENGLAND**
GRAHAM SUTHERLAND 1903-
VICTOR PASMORE 1908-
FRANCIS BACON 1910-
ALAN DAVIE 1920-

**FRANCE**
CLAUDE MONET 1840-1926
PIERRE BONNARD 1867-1947
ÉDOUARD VUILLARD 1868-1940
HENRI MATISSE 1869-1954
GEORGES ROUAULT 1871-1958
FRANCIS PICABIA 1879-1953
ANDRÉ DERAIN 1880-1954
ALBERT GLEIZES 1881-1953
FERNAND LÉGER 1881-1955
GEORGES BRAQUE 1882-1963
LOUIS MARCOUSSIS 1883-1941
JEAN METZINGER 1883-1956
MARCEL DUCHAMP 1887-1968
ANDRÉ MASSON 1896-
YVES TANGUY 1900-1955
BALTHUS (BALTHASAR KLOSSOWSKY) 1908-
NICOLAS DE STAËL 1914-1955
PIERRE SOULAGES 1919-

**SCANDINAVIA**
EDVARD MUNCH (NORWEGIAN) 1863-1944

**EASTERN EUROPE**
FRANK KUPKA (CZECH) 1871-1957
OSCAR KOKOSCHKA (AUSTRIAN) 1886-

**RUSSIA**
WASSILY KANDINSKY 1866-1944
CASIMIR MALEVICH 1878-1935
ANTOINE PEVSNER 1886-1962
MARC CHAGALL 1887-
NAUM GABO 1890-1966
CHAIM SOUTINE 1894-1943

**LATIN AMERICA**
JOSÉ CLEMENTE OROZCO (MEXICAN) 1883-1949
DIEGO RIVERA (MEXICAN) 1886-1957
DAVID SIQUEIROS (MEXICAN) 1898-1974
RUFINO TAMAYO (MEXICAN) 1899-
ROBERTO MATTA ECHAURREN (CHILEAN) 1912-

# Bibliography

* Also available in paperback.
† Only available in paperback.

Amaya, Mario, *Pop Art . . . And After.* The Viking Press, 1965.

Barr, Alfred H., Jr., ed., *Painting and Sculpture in the Museum of Modern Art.* Simon and Schuster, 1948.

Battcock, Gregory, *Minimal Art: A Critical Anthology.** E. P. Dutton & Co., Inc., 1968.

Baur, John I. H., ed., *New Art in America.* Frederick A. Praeger, 1957.

Baur, John I. H., *Revolution and Tradition in Modern American Art.** Harvard University Press, 1966.

Benton, Thomas Hart, *An Artist in America.* University of Missouri Press, 1968.

Brion, Marcel, and others, *Art Since 1945.** Harry N. Abrams, 1958.

Brown, Milton W.:
*American Painting from the Armory Show to the Depression.* Princeton University Press, 1955.
*The Story of the Armory Show.* The Joseph Hirshhorn Foundation, 1963.

Eliot, Alexander, *Three Hundred Years of American Painting.* Time Inc., 1957.

Geldzahler, Henry:
*American Painting in the Twentieth Century.* The Metropolitan Museum of Art, 1965.
*New York Painting and Sculpture: 1940-1970.** E. P. Dutton & Co., Inc., 1969.

Getlein, Frank, *Jack Levine.* Harry N. Abrams, 1966.

Glackens, Ira, *William Glackens and the Ashcan Group.*† Grosset & Dunlap, 1957.

Goodrich, Lloyd, and John I. H. Baur, *American Art of Our Century.* Frederick A. Praeger, 1961.

Hunter, Sam, *Modern Painting and Sculpture.*† Dell Publishing Co., Inc., 1969.

Kootz, Samuel M., *Modern American Painters.* Brewer & Warren, Inc., 1930.

Kuh, Katharine, *The Artist's Voice.* Harper & Row, 1962.

Larkin, Oliver W., *Art and Life in America.* Holt, Rinehart and Winston, 1966.

Lippard, Lucy R., *Pop Art.** Frederick A. Praeger, 1966.

McCoubrey, John W.:
*American Art: 1700-1960.*† Prentice-Hall, 1965.
*American Tradition in Painting.* George Braziller, 1963.

McLanathan, Richard, *The American Tradition in the Arts.* Harcourt, Brace & World, Inc., 1968.

Matthews, J. H., *An Introduction to Surrealism.* The Pennsylvania State University Press, 1965.

O'Conner, Francis V., *Jackson Pollock.** The Museum of Modern Art, 1967.

Perlman, Bernard B., *The Immortal Eight: American Painting from Eakins to the Armory Show.* Exposition Press, 1962.

Rodman, Selden, *Conversations with Artists.*† Capricorn Books, 1961.

Rose, Barbara, *American Art Since 1900: A Critical History.** Frederick A. Praeger, 1967.

Rose, Barbara, ed., *Readings in American Art Since 1900: A Documentary Survey.* Frederick A. Praeger, 1968.

Rublowsky, John, *Pop Art.* Basic Books, Inc., 1965.

Russell, John, and Suzi Gablik, *Pop Art Redefined.** Frederick A. Praeger, 1969.

Selz, Peter, *Seven Decades: 1895-1965, Crosscurrents in Modern Art.* Public Education Association, 1966.

# Acknowledgments

For their help in the production of this book the editors wish to thank the following people: Leon Arkus, Curator, Carnegie Institute of Art, Pittsburgh; Charles L. Decker, Manager, Veterans Memorial Building, Cedar Rapids; Ira Glackens; Budd Hopkins; Denny Judson, Whitney Museum of American Art, New York; Peter A. Juley & Son, New York; Russell Lynes; Robert Natkin; John Russell; Pierre Schneider; Mrs. John Sloan; Raphael Soyer; Richard Tooke, Museum of Modern Art, New York.

# Picture Credits

*The sources for the illustrations in this book appear below. Credits for pictures from left to right are separated by semicolons, from top to bottom by dashes.*

SLIPCASE: David Lees for TIME.

FRONT ENDPAPER, BACK ENDPAPER AND FRONTISPIECE: Marlborough Gallery Inc., New York

CHAPTER 1: 12—Jahn & Ollier for LIFE. 15—Sloan Collection, Delaware Art Center. 16—Sloan Collection, Delaware Art Center (2) —Courtesy Ira Glackens. 19—Sloan Collection, Delaware Art Center. 21—Whitney Museum of American Art, New York, photo by Geoffrey Clements. 22, 23—New York Public Library. 24—Chapellier Gallery, New York. 25—The Art Institute of Chicago. 26, 27 —Kraushaar Galleries, New York; The Wadsworth Atheneum, Hartford, Connecticut. 28, 29—Addison Gallery of American Art, Phillips Academy, Andover, Massachusetts. 30, 31—The Cleveland Museum of Art. 32—The Metropolitan Museum of Art. 33—Lee Boltin. 34—The Brooklyn Museum—Lee Boltin. 35—Eric Schaal.

CHAPTER 2: 36—Frank Lerner for TIME. 40—Kurt Severin from Black Star. 43—Archives of American Art. 45—Robert S. Crandall for TIME. 46—Whitney Museum of American Art, New York, photo by Geoffrey Clements. 47—Eric Schaal for LIFE. 48—Frank Lerner for TIME. 49—Whitney Museum of American Art, New York. 50, 51—© The Museum of Modern Art, New York; Philadelphia Museum of Art, photo by A. J. Wyatt. 52, 53—Whitney Museum of American Art, New York, photo by Geoffrey Clements; Eric Schaal for TIME. 54—Herbert Orth for LIFE. 55—Whitney Museum of American Art, New York, photo by Geoffrey Clements. 56—Frank Lerner for TIME. 57—Fogg Art Museum, Harvard University. 58, 59—© The Museum of Modern Art, New York; Walker Art Center, Minneapolis, Minnesota.

CHAPTER 3: 60—Herbert Orth for LIFE. 63—Alfred Eisenstaedt from PIX, Inc. 65—Harris & Ewing from Gilloon Agency. 66—Wide World. 69, 70, 71—Peter A. Juley & Son for FORTUNE. 72—John Savage. 73—Photo courtesy Whitney Museum of American Art, New York. 74, 75—Lee Boltin. 76, 77—The Art Institute of Chicago. 78, 79—© Associated American Artists. 80, 81—Fernand Bourges for LIFE. 82, 83—A.C.A. Galleries, New York. 84—Whitney Museum of American Art, New York. 85, 86, 87—© The Museum of Modern Art, New York. 88 through 91—Robert S. Crandall for TIME.

CHAPTER 4: 92—Yale Joel for LIFE. 94—Library of Congress (2)— Resettlement Administration. 95—Resettlement Administration (2) —Library of Congress. 99—Drawings by Jack Levine. 101—Valentine Gallery. 102, 103—Eric Schaal. 104, 105—The University of Nebraska. 106, 107—Robert S. Crandall for TIME. 108, 109— Whitney Museum of American Art, New York, photo by Geoffrey Clements; Henry Beville. 110 through 113—© The Museum of Modern Art, New York. 114, 115—Whitney Museum of American Art, New York, photo by Geoffrey Clements.

CHAPTER 5: 116—M. Knoedler & Co., Inc., New York. 118—George Platt Lynes photo courtesy Russell Lynes. 125—Frank Lerner for TIME. 126—Lee Boltin. 127, 128, 129—Whitney Museum of American Art, New York, photos by Geoffrey Clements. 130, 131—Whitney Museum of American Art, New York. 132—Lee Boltin. 133— Whitney Museum of American Art, New York, photo by Geoffrey Clements. 134, 135—Whitney Museum of American Art, New York; © The Museum of Modern Art, New York.

CHAPTER 6: 136—Frank Lerner for TIME. 139—Collection Mr. & Mrs. Herbert Benevy, New York. 142—Rudolph Burkhardt—Martha Holmes for LIFE. 145 through 147—Frank Lerner for TIME. 148, 149—Frank Lerner for TIME except upper right Whitney Museum of American Art, New York. 150, 151—Whitney Museum of American Art, New York. 152—Frank Lerner for TIME. 153— Eric Schaal for TIME. 154—© The Museum of Modern Art, New York. 155, 156, 157—Frank Lerner for TIME. 158—Herbert Orth for LIFE. 159—M. Knoedler & Co., Inc., New York, photo by Paulus Leeser.

CHAPTER 7: 160—J. R. Eyerman for TIME. 166—Steve Schapiro for LIFE; Walter Bennett for TIME. 167—Henri Dauman for LIFE. 169 —Foto Ann Münchow. 170, 171—David Lees for TIME. 172—David Lees. 173—Walker Art Center, Minneapolis, Minnesota. 174 —Harry N. Abrams Collection. 175—Leo Castelli Collection. 176, 177—Albright-Knox Art Gallery, Buffalo, New York. 178—Whitney Museum of American Art, New York, photo by Geoffrey Clements. 179—Frank Lerner for TIME. 180—Cordier & Ekstrom, Inc., New York. 181—Foto Ann Münchow—Frank Lerner for TIME. 182— Whitney Museum of Art, New York. 183—Frank Lerner for TIME; Galerie Chalette, New York—Foto Ann Münchow; André Emmerich Gallery Inc., New York. 184—Photo courtesy Leo Castelli Gallery.

# Index

*Numerals in italics indicate a picture of the subject mentioned. Dimensions are given in inches; height precedes width.*

# Index (continued)

*The text for this book was set in Bodoni Book, a typeface that was named for its Italian designer, Giambattista Bodoni (1740-1813). One of the earliest modern typefaces, Bodoni Book differs from more evenly weighted old-style characters in the greater contrast between thick and thin parts of letters. The Bodoni character is vertical with a thin, straight serif.*

PRINTED IN U.S.A.

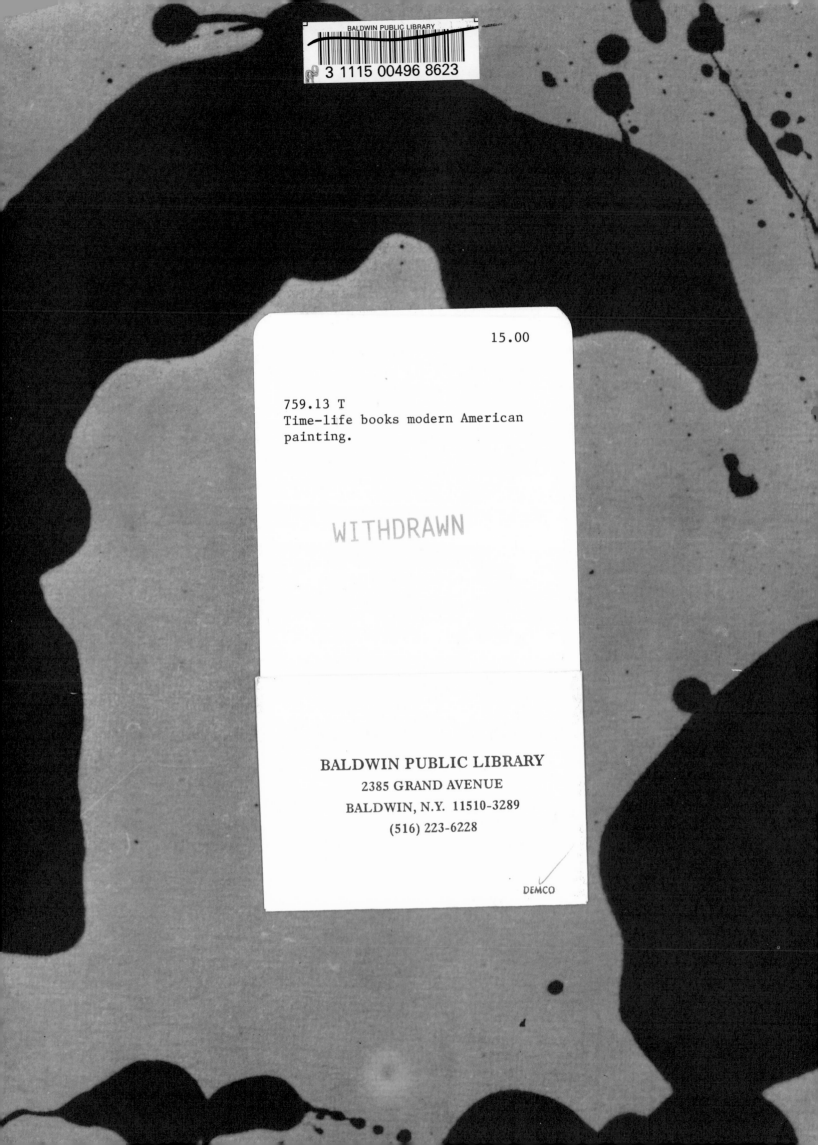